CURB THE CARB

CURB THE CARB

AMANDA CROSS

hamlyn

Notes

Standard level spoon measures are used in all recipes

1 tablespoon = one 15ml spoon

1 teaspoon = one 5ml spoon

Both metric and imperial measurements are given for the recipes. Use one set of measures only, not a mixture of both.

Ovens should be preheated to the specified temperature. If using a fan-assisted oven, follow the manufacturer's instructions for adjusting the time and temperature. Grills should also be preheated.

A few recipes include nuts and nut derivatives. Anyone with a known nut allergy must avoid these.

Free-range medium eggs should be used unless otherwise stated. The Department of Health advises that eggs should not be consumed raw. It is prudent for more vulnerable people, such as pregnant and nursing mothers, invalids, the elderly, babies and young children, to avoid uncooked or lightly cooked dishes made with eggs.

Meat and poultry should be cooked thoroughly. To test if poultry is cooked, pierce the flesh through the thickest part with a skewer or fork – the juices should run clear, never pink or red.

Fresh herbs should be used unless otherwise stated. If unavailable, use dried herbs as an alternative, but halve the quantities.

All the recipes in this book have been analyzed by the author. The analysis refers to each serving, unless otherwise stated.

First published in Great Britain in 2003 by
Hamlyn, a division of Octopus Publishing Group Ltd
2–4 Heron Quays, London E14 4JP

ISBN 0 600 60791 7

A CIP catalogue record for this book is available from the British Library

Printed and bound in China

10 9 8 7 6 5 4 3 2 1

Contents

Introduction

So you've picked up yet another diet book, in the hope that this will be the one that makes all the difference. It can be – but not if you are aiming for a quick fix, only to return to the bad habits that got you here in the first place. There is no joy in yo-yo dieting; it makes you miserable, lowers your self-esteem and makes you view food as the enemy, not as an enjoyable way of providing your body with the fuel it needs to remain healthy and disease-free.

Before we go any further, let's get one thing straight … I have been that yo-yo dieter – my weight has been up and down more times than the stock exchange. Periodically I have tried everything from low-fat to high-fibre diets; I have eaten more cabbage and grapefruit than I care to think about; paid out fortunes for dreadful-tasting drinks and so-called 'meal-replacement' bars; and even done the dreaded pill thing. What I am trying to tell you is that I understand the plight of those of you who have battled with weight for a long time and seem to be getting nowhere.

I am never going to be a paragon of virtue. I am just as likely as the next person to binge on a whole tub of ice cream and eat everything on offer at the hotel breakfast buffet. But I have learned to do it occasionally and not suffer undue guilt as a result. As long as most of my diet is healthy and doing me good, that's fine. And when I combine this approach with regular exercise, the results speak for themselves. But it has taken a long time to get to this point.

Looking back, I have never been the sort of person who ploughs into the sweet stuff. I would far rather have a chunk of cheese than a slice of cake. In theory, the bulk of my diet was one I considered quite healthy: a mixture of veg and fruit, complex carbohydrates and low-fat food, which I thought was doing me a power of good (even though I was constantly battling with my weight). I wasn't eating much protein (more for reasons of laziness than political correctness or conscience), although if I felt below par, I craved homemade chicken soup or a big salmon steak. However, I began to notice that every time I tucked into pasta or ate my way through a plate of sandwiches, my stomach would blow up like a balloon, followed by sleepiness and – more frighteningly – the desire to eat even more carb-laden snacks. I was becoming a carbohydrate junkie.

So a couple of years ago I experimented with raising my protein levels and cutting down on the carbs, by trying the Atkins diet, which is based on the principle of ketosis as a method of burning fat (see page 52). I managed to lose about 4.5kg (10lb) in two weeks, but I felt the diet was too restrictive for

Burger and fries is a carb-heavy dish that is usually full of hydrogenated fats and poor quality meat.

me and seemed to license me to eat large amounts of saturated fat. After another year of suffering the same symptoms, I decided to try a different approach. I gave up wheat and anything processed or refined, increased my levels of protein again, ate salads every day and didn't stint on the olive oil. The weight just started to fall away: 13kg (28lb) of excess flab went in a relatively short time, and has stayed off ever since. This wasn't due to cutting out carbohydrates altogether, just 'curbing the carb'; I was simply more selective about the type of carbohydrates I was eating, and I had changed the balance of my diet to include more protein and healthy fats.

I couldn't help noticing that high-protein diets were plastered all over the press: any celebrity who had lost weight seemed to be following that type of regime. I had lost weight easily doing just that, but how was my approach different from the diet I had tried a couple of years before? I decided to do a bit of research and look into the whole high-protein/low-carb topic with fresh eyes.

Dr Atkins was one of the early pioneers, but even though there were certain strengths in his way of thinking, his dietary approach was extreme. Things have moved on a lot since then, and the way in which he and others now tackle this issue has taken on a far more holistic, healthy slant.

Leslie Kenton, one of the most respected gurus in the field of health and nutrition, has shed new light on the subject. In *The X Factor Diet* she discusses a condition called Syndrome X, otherwise known as insulin resistance (see page 17). This is the collective name for a group of metabolic conditions that can predispose us to obesity, high blood pressure, diabetes and heart disease. First discovered in 1988 by Gerald Reaven, an endocrinologist at California's Stanford University, insulin resistance is now believed by many scientists to affect approximately two-thirds of the adult population in the Western world. If you are addicted to carbohydrates, to eating a diet that is high in refined and processed food and low in fat, have difficulty losing weight and suffer from any of the symptoms given in the table (see right), you could be one of those people.

Even though your motivation for losing weight may be primarily aesthetic, it's your health that really counts – that should spur you on.

This book is about attitudes, re-education and changing your eating habits for life. It starts with a look at the basics of nutrition, then offers advice on how

LONG-TERM EFFECTS OF INSULIN RESISTANCE

- ◆ **Raised insulin levels, leading to insulin resistance**
- ◆ **Lowered metabolic rate, leading to weight gain**
- ◆ **Increased fat tissue and reduced muscle**
- ◆ **Accelerated biological ageing**
- ◆ **Increased food allergies and intolerances**
- ◆ **Overworked immune system**
- ◆ **Increased risk of heart disease, obesity, diabetes and cancer**

If you have a problem with insulin resistance you should cut down on complex carbohydrates and increase your intake of fibrous colourful vegetables.

- ◆ **Successful weight management**
- ◆ **Increased energy levels**
- ◆ **More efficient immune system**
- ◆ **Balanced insulin levels**
- ◆ **Stabilized blood sugar**
- ◆ **Reduced risk of degenerative conditions such as cancer, diabetes, heart disease.**
- ◆ **Slower biological ageing**
- ◆ **Fat reduction**
- ◆ **Fewer mood swings and cravings**
- ◆ **Enhanced concentration and performance**

to diet successfully on a low-carb diet. The rest of the book presents three dietary stages to follow – the Fast-Track Plan, the Keep on Tracking Plan and the No Backtracking Plan – each of which incorporates general principles and rules, plus a wide range of enticing recipes – and a section on how to adapt these plans for a vegetarian diet.

Even though you may feel that reading all the 'technical stuff' is unimportant, I urge you to do so, because 'knowledge is power'. Don't follow everything I say blindly; think about some of the points discussed and get to know your own body. More importantly, get yourself back in the driving seat and get ready to shift some fat. You don't need it any more.

Take solace in the fact you are not alone: millions of people all over the world are (or should be) 'fighting the flab', as the next section of the book will illustrate.

Who needs to curb the carbs?

It goes without saying that everyone should consider cutting out refined sugar and flour products, plus high levels of processed foods that are full of junk fats, as they are nutritionally redundant in the human body. You should also consider giving up caffeine and moderating your alcohol intake, particularly if you suffer from any of the symptoms of unstable blood sugar and insulin resistance.

Many people are not even aware of the symptoms of eating too many refined and dense carbohydrates. They have become used to living in what I call 'the discomfort zone'. They have forgotten what it is like to wake up full of energy, think it's normal to feel bloated after meals and rely too heavily on stimulants such as coffee to get themselves through the day.

This sorry state of affairs becomes their normal state of being – it is no wonder that the symptoms of degenerative disease creep up on many people un-noticed. They are so used to living below their physical potential that they don't recognise the signs until it is sometimes too late.

If you are more genetically disposed to gain weight readily when exposed to an unhealthy diet and lifestyle then restricting the amount and type of carbohydrate foods that you eat may be the right choice for you. Such a diet regime may also suit you if you have developed insulin resistance as the result of a diet based on high levels of refined and complex carbohydrates that outweigh your energy requirements, plus too much saturated fat, with little fibre and water. Unless, that is, you are one of those people who leads an active lifestyle or has a high metabolic rate, and already eats a diet with relatively high levels of healthy complex carbohydrates (brown rice, potatoes, wholegrains and certain vegetables, fruit and pulses) without accompanying weight and health problems. If so, why are you reading this book? Sounds like you are already doing what is right for your body.

Nutrit

ion

Globesity

We live in a world where half the population seems to be obsessed by dieting, while the other half is suffering from starvation and malnutrition. We have no control over the natural disasters that leave millions fighting to find enough food to survive, but why is it that so many people – not just in the Western world, but also in developing countries – are becoming overweight, leading to soaring levels of diabetes, cardiovascular disease and certain cancers?

We may have made huge advances in technology, but we seem to have lost our connection to nature, and nowhere is this better illustrated than in the food we eat. Our meat is sold in sterile packaging, and contains antibiotics, growth hormones and pesticide residue. We eat (well, some of us eat) fruit and vegetables that are sprayed, waxed, dyed and sometimes irradiated to make them look attractive. The grains that form the bulk of many

THE RISKS FROM OBESITY

Being overweight can induce:
- ◆ **Diabetes (type 2: non-insulin-dependent, see page 15)**
- ◆ **Coronary heart disease and strokes.**

It increases the risks of:
- ◆ **Cancer of the colon, prostate, uterus, cervix, breasts and ovaries**
- ◆ **Gall-bladder disease**
- ◆ **Musculoskeletal disorders and respiratory problems.**

Fast-food is increasingly chosen as a convenient alternative to healthy home-cooking with naturally grown produce.

94 per cent of Americans eat pizza. They consume three billion per year, which is the equivalent of 100 acres of pizza per day – roughly 350 pizzas per second!

people's diets are stripped of their fibre and nutrient content. And the milk we drink is pasteurized.

Because there is so much choice, so little time and sometimes so little money, many people choose the convenient pre-packaged or fast-food option, rather than insisting on good-quality, naturally produced, locally available produce. They would rather sit and watch a cookery programme on television while eating a TV dinner or a take-out than get into the kitchen and cook a healthy meal for themselves.

According to the World Health Organization (WHO), in 1995 there were an estimated 200 million obese adults worldwide, and by 2000 that figure had increased to 300 million. But obesity is not just a problem restricted to adults – 25 per cent of children and adolescents in the US are overweight. The problem is beginning to replace malnutrition and infectious diseases as the most significant contributor to ill health worldwide. Obesity is now recognized as a disease in its own right, but one that is largely preventable through changes in lifestyle – especially diet.

THE PRIMARY CAUSES OF OBESITY

◆ Sedentary lifestyles, where energy intake is higher than energy expenditure
◆ Energy-dense diets that are excessively high in refined sugars and flour, plus junk fats, and lacking in fibre and essential nutrients
◆ Continual crash dieting

A lesson from dietary history

For years we have been fed the information that a low-fat/high-carbohydrate diet is the healthiest one for us. The ideal ratio, based on our calorie intake, is 55 per cent carbs, 15 per cent protein and 30 per cent fats. This ratio may work for some individuals, but it certainly isn't right for everyone, particularly those whose carbohydrate intake is based on the wrong sort of carbs (see page 18).

One of the most thought-provoking arguments for reducing the amount and type of carbohydrates that we eat is the story of Palaeolithic people. Genetically, there is very little difference between ourselves and our hunter-gatherer ancestors, although our diet has certainly changed.

Palaeolithic people were treading the Earth thousands of years before we started to cultivate crops and rear animals for food, and according to scientists they existed on a diet that was primarily protein. Between 60 and 90 per cent of their diet consisted of game animals, eggs, birds, reptiles and insects. The rest comprised green leafy vegetables and berries. Obviously they were leading a far more active life than the average 21st-century human being, but their diet must have been in part responsible for their healthy bones, flawless teeth and good musculature.

It was only at around the time of the agricultural revolution, about 10,000 years ago, that we started to rely on starchy vegetables such as potatoes and cereal crops for the bulk of our diet, and lifestyles became more sedentary. By 4,000 years ago the effects of the change in diet were beginning to be seen in the human body:

- ◆ There was a reduction in people's stature
- ◆ Dental decay and malformation of the jaw had become widespread
- ◆ Disease and epidemics were starting to shorten the human lifespan.

Warning signs from the present day

- ◆ 300,000 American deaths per year are due to obesity-related non-communicable diseases. This accounts for 12 per cent of the entire US healthcare expenditure, costing the country $100 billion (£70 billion) per year. The cost of a cheeseburger may be coming down, but its cost to the nation's health most certainly is not.
- ◆ In 2002 the Centre for Disease Control and Prevention (CDC) in Atlanta estimated that 17 million Americans, including 151,000 under the age of 20, now have diabetes. Type 2 (or adult-onset) diabetes is a disorder resulting from the body's inability to make enough insulin (a hormone that regulates glucose metabolism in the body) – and it can be life-threatening. The risks of heart disease and stroke increase two- to fourfold and the death rate doubles in diabetics. The disease is also the leading cause of blindness, kidney failure and amputations.

WHY WERE PALAEOLITHIC PEOPLE SO HEALTHY?

- ◆ **They had an active lifestyle**
- ◆ **Their protein intake was far higher in polyunsaturated fats, because their animals were smaller and wild**
- ◆ **Their consumption of fibre was far higher than ours, at around 100g (3½oz) per day**
- ◆ **The plants and berries they were eating were providing them with around 300 times more immune-boosting and antioxidant phytonutrients (plant nutrients) and vitamin C than the average diet offers today.**

◆ In 2002 the National Audit Office in the UK revealed the following facts: 58 per cent of adults in the UK are technically overweight, and 20 per cent are clinically obese (with a BMI of over 30 per cent, see page 42).

In 1998 around 30,000 people in England alone died prematurely as a direct consequence of being overweight.

In the same year obesity was responsible for 1.8 million lost working days, costing the National Health Service and the economy of the country an estimated £2.5 billion ($3.6 billion).

The number of people who are obese in England has tripled over the last 20 years, and if this trend continues, one in four people will be obese by the year 2010.

◆ North American Inuits, whose native diet traditionally consists of whale meat, berries and moss, had no history of heart disease, diabetes or dental decay – until they introduced white flour and sugar into their diets.

Maintaining a normal weight is a constant battle for many individuals. Continual yo-yo dieting can lead to clinical complications and shatter a person's self-esteem.

The carb connection

Carbohydrates are a vital part of the human diet – they are our primary source of energy, and in their natural state they are turned into glucose to provide fuel for all the organs of the body.

THERE ARE THREE MAIN TYPES OF CARBOHYDRATES:
1. Simple sugars, or monosaccharides: glucose (blood sugar), and fructose (fruit sugar)
2. Double sugars, or disaccharides: lactose (milk sugar)
3. Complex carbohydrates, or polysaccharides: starches and cellulose (potatoes, rice, grains and dietary fibre).

The simplest carbohydrate of them all is glucose, which is assimilated immediately by the body. The more complex the carbohydrate's structure, the longer it takes the body to convert it into energy – so 'complex' carbohydrates are the slow burners, because they are higher in more complicated sugars and fibre and thus take longer to break down into energy-giving glucose.

Milk contains lactose – the only carbohydrate source that doesn't come from fruits, vegetables and grains.

So why are carbs the bad guys?

Even though carbohydrates are a vital component of our overall health, there are certain carbs that serve no nutritional purpose whatsoever, and can even cause us harm if consumed too regularly and in large proportions. They are also the main contributors to the escalating obesity problem. So who are these enemies of our health and weight? They are known as refined carbohydrates.

The problems started the minute we began to process our food and strip out the fibre and nutrients from flour and sugar, to make them look appealingly white. In so doing, we made them nutritionally redundant. Food processing removes magnesium, zinc and chromium from flour and sugar – the three minerals that the body needs to metabolize carbohydrates properly. It also drastically reduces vitamins B_1, B_2, B_3, calcium and iron.

Junk foods made up of refined flour and sugar, plus nutritionally empty processed fats, colourings, flavourings and preservatives, make up 75 per cent of many people's diets. These so-called 'convenience foods' are 'empty' calories, which hurtle into the bloodstream, play havoc with insulin and blood-sugar levels and actually deplete the body of essential vitamins and minerals that are needed to perform other important bodily functions. Processed foods have also been stripped of their fibre content, which is essential for controlling insulin production and protecting the body against diseases such as diverticulitis and colon cancer.

The link between carbohydrates and insulin resistance

The hormone insulin plays a major role in the metabolism of carbohydrates and their conversion to energy in the body. When you eat carbohydrates, they are converted into glucose in the bloodstream, which triggers the release of insulin. This virtually escorts the glucose to the body's cells, where it can be used as energy. If there is too much glucose, the insulin turns it into glycogen, which is stored in your muscles and liver ready to be converted back to glucose when it is needed.

However, in the high-refined 'carb' world in which we live, we often have too much glucose floating around in the bloodstream, and then insulin converts it to fat. And our body cells may become so flooded with insulin that they cease to be responsive to it, so the pancreas keeps producing more and more insulin in an attempt to get energy to your cells. This is known as 'insulin resistance'.

For many in the western world, 75 per cent of their diet is based on refined carbohydrates that have had their vitamins, minerals and fibre stripped away.

ARE YOU INSULIN-RESISTANT?

These symptoms can all be indicative of unstable blood-sugar levels:

◆ **Fatigue**
◆ **Mood swings**
◆ **Brain fog and an inability to function at your best**
◆ **A craving for carbohydrates, followed by a feeling of bloatedness and dizziness after eating them**
◆ **Constant hunger**
◆ **Continual yo-yo dieting, without ever shifting excess fat.**

If many of these symptoms apply to you, then it is time to go into dietary 'rehab'. It sounds as if you are a carbohydrate junkie.

Over a period of time, less and less glucose gets used as energy, and more and more gets laid down as fat. Since insulin also sends messages to the brain to tell you that you are hungry, more and more insulin means increasing cravings for carb-laden food.

The only people who are benefiting from refined foods are:

◆ The dentists who have to patch up your decaying teeth

◆ The pharmaceutical companies who have to sell you drugs to sort out the symptoms of your ailing immune system and your susceptibility to chronic and degenerative disease

◆ The food manufacturers, who are only really interested in profit.

If you add to this a high intake of caffeine, alcohol, smoking and a lack of exercise, then you will almost certainly be taking a wobbly walk down the road to ill health.

Diets based on lean protein, healthy fats and fibrous vegetables will have a profound effect on your health and energy levels.

Is it enough just to cut out refined carbohydrates?

Totally banishing all things processed and adopting a healthier diet based on fresh produce is a definite start, but if you have a weight problem linked to insulin resistance, it may not be enough, because if you are still eating a diet that is too high in the wrong sort of carbohydrates – coupled with not eating enough protein or fat to slow down the rate at which these excessive carbs are hitting your blood-sugar levels – you will still have problems. A low-fat/high-carb diet can give you a nasty shock every time you jump on the scales.

Rice is full of refined carbohydrates and should be completely cut out of your diet.

THE EMPTY CALORIES OF
REFINED CARBOHYDRATES

Have a quick look through the following list and see if it rings any alarm bells. If your diet includes a large proportion of these foods, don't just curb them – *cut them out altogether.*

White bread and bread products

White rice

Refined sugar

Salt

Fizzy drinks

Bottled cordials and juice 'drinks'

Sweets

Chocolate

Margarine

Sweet biscuits and cakes

Crisps and salted nuts

Canned fruit and vegetables

Processed meat products,
    such as burgers and sausages

Sugary cereals

Sweet-fruit low-fat yogurts

Ice cream and ice lollies

White pasta

Pre-packaged convenience meals

Sauces and gravy mixes

Take-out foods, such as pizza and
    Chinese meals

The thing to remember is that all carbohydrates have an effect on your blood sugar, and every gram of carbohydrate consumed is equal to one gram of glucose in your bloodstream. So if you are eating more than your body can burn for energy, or can safely store as glycogen in the liver, the rest will be turned to fat.

The key factor in balancing blood-sugar levels and banishing the symptoms of insulin resistance is controlling your intake of carbohydrates. In order to do this effectively you need to know which ones have the greatest impact on your blood sugar and which do not.

Initially, this will need a little time and effort on your part as you learn about the different sorts of carbohydrates. You may find that the changes you have to make to your diet are quite drastic, but before long – as you start to feel and look better – you will be amazed at how little you miss the wrong kinds of carbohydrates such as processed and sugary foods. You won't feel the need to pile your plate high with potatoes and pasta, because your newly balanced blood sugar levels won't be crying out for a carbohydrate fix.

FRIGHTENING FACTS

According to figures from the most recent Federal Continuing Survey of Food Intakes by Individuals (1994–6), the average American eats the equivalent of 20 teaspoons of sugar a day. Nearly 60 per cent of this intake, says the trade group the Sugar Association, comes from corn sweeteners, which are heavily used in sodas and other sweetened drinks. The other 40 per cent comes from sucrose (table sugar), with a small amount from other sweeteners, such as honey and molasses.

Becoming a GI Joe

All carbohydrates have a value on what is known as the 'glycaemic index' (GI), which indicates how quickly that carbohydrate is metabolized by the body and converted into glucose. The lower a food's GI, the longer it takes to be converted. Foods with the highest GIs are the ones that will have the most profound and immediate effect on your blood-sugar levels. All the carbohydrates on a weight-loss and insulin-balancing regime should come from the lower ranges.

There are two indexes: the glucose standard, which rates glucose as having a GI of 100 and the white bread standard, which is based on white bread being equal to 100. Other carbohydrates are assigned comparative ratios based on these figures. It doesn't really matter which index you adhere to, for they both give a pretty good – and sometimes surprising – insight into the speed with which certain carbohydrates are assimilated into the bloodstream.

Below are a few GI values of common foods, based on the glucose standard. Of course you are not expected to remember each specific food's value, so to make things easier, opposite are two simple tables showing you how to classify fruit and vegetables into those with a low GI value (under 20), those with a medium value (20–60) and those with a high value (over 60).

THE GLUCOSE STANDARD: SAMPLE VALUES

Food	GI value	Food	GI value
Glucose	100	Peas	51
Baked potato	98	Ice cream	50
Cooked carrots	92	Rye bread	42
Honey	92	Pasta	41
Instant white rice	91	Apples	39
Cornflakes	84	Plain yogurt	38
White bread	72	Chickpeas	36
Wholewheat bread	69	Strawberries	32
Table sugar	64	Tomatoes	28
Raisins	61	Peaches	26
Oatmeal	61	Cherries	24
Pitta bread	57	Fructose	20
Popcorn	55	Soya beans	15
Banana	53	Peanuts	13
Potato crisps	51	Channa dahl (lentils)	7

LOW GI VEGETABLES

asparagus, bean sprouts, beet greens, broccoli, cabbage, cauliflower, celery, cucumber, endive, lettuce, mustard greens, radishes, spinach, Swiss chard, watercress

MEDIUM GI VEGETABLES

aubergine, beets, Brussels sprouts, chives, collards, dandelion leaves, greens, kale, kohlrabi, leeks, okra, onions, parsley, peas, peppers, pimento, pumpkin, rutabagas, string beans, turnips

HIGH GI VEGETABLES

artichokes, carrot, corn, dried beans, lima beans, oyster plant, parsnips, potato, squash, sweet potato, yam

LOW GI FRUIT

cantaloupe, rhubarb, watermelon

MEDIUM GI FRUIT

apples, fresh apricots, bananas, blackberries, cherries, cranberries, grapefruit, guava, kiwis, lemons, limes, oranges, papayas, peaches, plums, raspberries, strawberries, tangerines, tomatoes

HIGH GI FRUIT

any dried fruit, blueberries, figs, grapes, kumquats, loganberries, mangoes, mulberries, pears, pineapple, pomegranates, prunes

Add finely chopped, raw vegetables to dishes at the last minute to maximize on their phytonutrient, vitamin and mineral content.

Density values

Each carbohydrate can also be evaluated by its density value. This is the amount of usable carbohydrate in relation to fibre and water content – the more fibre and water a vegetable or fruit contains, the less usable carbohydrates it will have. The most dense carbohydrate foods are pulses, wholegrains and starchy vegetables, particularly when they are cooked and their fibre is broken down, these will raise your insulin levels, so always be aware of this. The table opposite contains a list of low-density carbohydrates that should form the basis of your carb intake on a low-carb diet.

Not only do many fruits feature highly on the GI scale, but a few should also carry a carbohydrate density warning sign. Bananas, dried fruit and concentrated fruit juices are all a bad idea if you are trying to balance your blood sugar levels. It is best to avoid these totally until your blood sugar and weight have normalized, and then carefully re-introduce them into your diet.

Focus on fibrous vegetables that can be eaten raw or steamed – the type that lose a lot of water whilst cooking. This will mean increasing your intake of leafy green vegetables, such as Swiss chard, green cabbage, kale, bok choy, rocket, spinach and endive.

Think back to the diet of out hunter-gatherer ancestors, they relied heavily on wild leaves and freshly picked berries to provide them with that all-important fibre and phytonutrients (see page 14).

This change to your diet will have a great impact on your digestive system as raw fibrous vegetables are eliminated far more quickly than processed carbohydrates that have had their fibre and nutrients removed.

 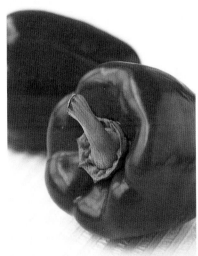 

DENSITY VALUES OF COMMON CARBOHYDRATES

Less than 1g of carbohydrate

125g (4oz) alfalfa sprouts 0.4g
75g (2½oz) sliced bok choy 0.8g
1 stick celery 0.9g
40g (1½oz) sliced endive 0.8g
75g (2½oz) shredded lettuce 0.4g
40g (1½oz) sliced radicchio 0.9g
5 radishes 0.8g
40g (1½oz) rocket 0.4g

Less than 3g of carbohydrate

6 fresh asparagus spears 2.4 g
50g (2oz) raw beetroot tops 1.8g
50g (2oz) blackberries 2.9g
175g (6oz) chopped raw broccoli 2.2g
175g (6oz) cauliflower florets 2.6g
½ medium cucumber 3g
40g (1½oz) chopped leeks 2g
60g (2½oz) boiled, sliced marrow 2.6g
40g (1½oz) sliced raw mushrooms 1.1g
90g (3oz) cooked mushrooms 2.3g
40g (1½oz) chopped parsley 1.9g
90g (3oz) chopped red pepper 2.4g
75g (2½oz) chopped raw spring
    onion 2.5g

Less than 5g of carbohydrates

125g (4oz) diced aubergine 4g
½ medium avocado 3.7g
25g (1oz) blueberries 4.3g
4 Brussels sprouts 3.4g
200g (7oz) red or green cabbage 3.6g
40g (1½oz) chopped dandelion leaves
    3.3g
50g (2oz) chopped fresh fennel 3.1g
75g (2½oz) sliced French beans 3.8g
75g (2½oz) mustard greens 4g
1 whole chilli pepper 4.3g
100g (3½oz) strawberries 3.3g
40g (1½oz) chopped Swiss chard 3.6g
1 medium tomato 4.3g
75g (2½oz) canned water chestnuts 4.5g

The carbohydrate jewels

By upping your intake of low GI fruit and vegetables (see page 21), you will not only be on your way to becoming leaner, but you will have a profound effect on your health. The amazing phytonutrients (plant nutrients) that you find in brightly coloured raw organic fruit and vegetables are clever little substances that can protect you from ill health in various ways, although many people's diets are sadly lacking in them.

Phytonutrients can help regulate the immune system, stabilize vitamins in body tissues and protect from serious illnesses, such as such as cancer. They do this by working as antioxidants alongside vitamins A, C, E and D, and the minerals, selenium and zinc. As a team, these powerful compounds have the ability to slow down the damaging oxidative process caused by those 'enemies of a healthy state', the free radicals. Antioxidants can also rid the body of these free radicals, which are the natural waste products of metabolism, which, if left unchecked, can lead to degenerative disease, by causing imbalances on a cellular level.

Take note that these free radicals are also found in overheated oils and fried foods, another good reason to kiss junk food good bye.

They aren't classed as essential nutrients, but without phytonutrients your sense of wellness would be severely compromised.

They work in the body at deep physiological and biochemical levels, and luckily enough are to be found in low-density/low GI fruit and vegetables. Eating these raw wherever possible is the key to maximizing their life-enhancing qualities. Cooking destroys many of the benefits that you will reap if you include a colourful array of energy-boosting raw fruit and vegetables in your daily diet.

Life is a balancing act

So now you have a better understanding of the impact that the wrong carbohydrates can have on your body, and have established that you need to incorporate more of the colourful and low GI fibrous fruit and vegetables in your diet. But man cannot live by carbohydrates alone. You will have to take a close look at the two other macronutrients that work hand-in-hand with carbohydrates to provide energy and nourish the body: protein (see pages 26–29) and fats (see pages 30–33).

The key to balancing blood-sugar levels, banishing insulin resistance and losing excess weight lies in successfully balancing these three macronutrients.

TEAMWORK

If your carbohydrates were a team, you would want to field your best players to ensure a great performance, so utilize these same tactics in your diet and improve your chances of victory.

Star players

Or should we say: the under-20s. All low GI fruit and vegetables, which score well below 20 on the GI scale and are full of fibre and life-enhancing phytonutrients. Maximize their raw talent.

On the bench

Be careful about how you play the higher-density quick-release carbs, which have passed the over-50 mark. Too many of these on the team and they will slow you down, unless you are very physically active.

Retired for life

How did these carbs ever get into the team in the first place? Wave goodbye to all those refined carbohydrates and processed foods.

Magical phytonutrients and their benefits

Phytonutrients	source	Benefits
Allyl sulfide	Garlic and onions	The allicin in these vegetables is a potent antiviral and antibacterial agent. It decreases the risk of stomach and colon cancer, lowers LDL (Low-Density Lipoproteins, or poor cholesterol), and encourages production of the enzyme glutathione S-transferase, which helps eliminate toxins from the body.
Lutein	Green leafy vegetables, spinach, turnip, beetroot tops, collard greens, kale, yellow marrow and squash	This carotene antioxidant protects against degenerative diseases and promotes healthy eyesight. It also protects all body cells from premature ageing.
Indoles, sulforaphanes	Broccoli, Brussels sprouts, cabbage, other leafy green vegetables	Indoles eliminate toxins, enhance immunity and prevent cancer-causing hormones from attaching themselves to cells. Sulforaphanes remove carcinogens (cancer-causing agents) from cells.
Isoflavones, such as saponins, phytosterols and genistein	Soya products	Isoflavones are powerful antioxidants that protect against cancer. Saponins enhance immune functions and help to prevent the absorption of cholesterol. Phytosterols lower cholesterol. Genistein prevents the body taking up dangerous chemical oestrogens.
Lycopene, P-coumaric acid, coumarins	Tomatoes, watermelon, pink grapefruit	From the same family as beta-carotene, lycopene has great antioxidant powers, guards against colon and bladder cancer, and reduces the risk of cardiovascular disease. P-coumaric acid inhibits the production of cancer-causing nitrosamines in the body. Coumarins reduce inflammation.
Limonene, glucarase	Citrus fruit: oranges, tangerines, grapefruits	Limonene enhances immunity and increases the production of anti-cancer enzymes. Glucarase eliminates degenerative chemicals from the body.
Alpha-carotene, beta-carotene	Orange vegetables and fruit: mangoes, pumpkins, carrots, sweet potatoes, squash, marrows	Alpha-carotene and beta-carotene are both antioxidants with a huge ability to boost immunity and decrease the risk of many cancers, degenerative disease and ageing.
Polyphenols, flavonoids	Berries, red grapes, red wine, artichokes, yams	These polyphenols lower the risk of heart disease and flush out chemicals. This group includes flavonoids which fight cell damage from oxidation, strengthen the blood vessels and capillaries.
Lignan precursors	Flaxseeds, linseeds	These prevent cancer, and are great sources of omega-3 fatty acids.

High-quality protein

Our bodies are composed mainly of protein, which (after water) is the most abundant substance in the body. It is the major constituent of our muscles, tissues, skin, hormones, enzymes, antibodies and blood. Even after childhood protein plays a vital role in maintaining and rebuilding our bodies as they cope with the wear and tear of daily life.

Proteins are broken down by the process of digestion into units called amino acids, and the body requires 22 amino acids to form human protein. All but nine can be produced in the body. These nine are known as 'essential amino acids' and have to be provided in the diet. Foods that contain all nine are termed 'complete proteins', and they include meat, fish, dairy and soya protein. Fruit, vegetables, grains and pulses are 'incomplete proteins' and have to be carefully combined to provide sufficient amino acids in the diet.

Protein is fundamental to rebalancing blood-sugar levels, because it encourages production of the hormone glucagon, which helps the body to release stored glycogen for energy and encourages the burning of fat. Glucagon also helps to balance excess insulin production.

ESSENTIAL AMINO ACIDS

These nine amino acids are not produced in the body, so we need to get them from the foods we eat:

◆ **Methionine**
◆ **Threonine**
◆ **Tryptophan**
◆ **Leucine**
◆ **Isoleucine**
◆ **Lysine**
◆ **Valine**
◆ **Phenylaline**
◆ **Histidine.**

Eggs are a fantastic source of protein and calcium and contain many essential nutrients such as zinc, iron and vitamin E.

What is Biological Value?

In order to be efficient, protein foods have to be of a high quality and have what is termed a high Biological Value (BV) – this indicates how much of the protein is retained by the body. Eggs used to be classed as having the highest BV, but micro-filtered whey, whey-peptide blends and lactalbumin (whey-protein concentrate) are even higher. Micro-filtered whey protein used to be a useless by-product of cheese manufacturing. Now it is processed at very low temperatures and turned into a protein source with a very high BV, that contains all essential and non-essential amino acids. If you assume that eggs represent 100 on the BV scale, then the figures look like this:

When it comes to meat and fish, buy the best you can afford – preferably wild, organic and lean.

Adding whey protein powder to smoothies is a great way of boosting protein levels.

BV RATINGS	
Whey-peptide blends and micro-filtered whey	110–59
Lactalbumin egg	104
Eggs	100
Cow's milk	91
Egg white	88
Beef	80
Fish	79
Chicken	79
Soya	74
Rice	59
Beans	49

The only whey to go

To maintain a healthy immune system, blood, skin and muscles, you need to consume protein with a high BV. Whey protein (which is derived from milk, see Q&A opposite) is an excellent supplement that has long been used by body-builders and athletes alike. It has many uses in a dietary regime:

◆ It encourages the formation of lean muscle mass
◆ It increases glutathione levels, which has great antioxidant and immune-boosting properties
◆ It helps to build healthy new collagen
◆ It provides an invaluable source of protein for vegetarians who are attempting to balance their diets
◆ It is a quick and easy way of having a high-protein meal or snack
◆ It can be incorporated into recipes as a replacement for carbohydrate ingredients.

There are a multitude of whey products on the market – some better than others. Many come in sweet flavours, which are great when making shakes and smoothies, but you need to source natural, unflavoured products if you want to incorporate whey-protein powder into savoury dishes such as soups. These are widely available through health-food stores and on the Web. Just make sure you don't confuse them with slimmer's meal-replacement powders, which are usually laden with carbohydrates.

The average serving of whey protein is a 25g (1oz) scoop, but check on the label to see how much of that scoop comprises protein: the lower the protein content, the higher the carbohydrate content. And beware of 'blends'; these are likely to be bulked up with milk and soya derivatives. To get the best out of your whey products, go for the highest protein concentration possible.

Whey protein powder contains more biologically available protein than fillet steak.

Soy beans contain isoflavones that are weak forms of plant oestrogens.

Soya's starring role

Soya is another star player on the protein front, and although it doesn't have as high a BV as whey protein, meat, fish or eggs, it has a multitude of health benefits which more than justify its inclusion in a low-carb diet; and it is a great vegetarian option.

Soya contains all-important isoflavones, which can reduce insulin levels, decrease arteriosclerosis (thickening of the arterial walls) and lower levels of LDL (Low-Density Lipoproteins, or poor cholesterol). It has also been shown to reduce the risk of osteoporosis (softening of the bones), increase bone mass and enhance the body's ability to retain calcium.

Soya is also of particular benefit to women, as the isoflavones it contains mimic the action of the female sex hormone oestrogen. It is believed that a diet high in soya can reduce the density of breast tissue, therefore lowering the risk of developing breast cancer.

Make it organic

The quality of the meat and fish we consume has dropped dramatically during the last century. Gone are the days when we were eating meat that came from animals allowed to graze freely on nutritious grass, and fish caught in unpolluted rivers and seas. Today, most farm animals are fed on grains that are high in carbohydrates and omega-6 fatty acids, then pumped full of antibiotics and hormones. And fish are being farmed in restrictive conditions, rendering them more fatty than their wild counterparts.

The only real answer is to buy the best that you can afford – the organic option being the healthiest and most nutritious. Organic is better because the quality of the food is better. It isn't loaded with drugs and hormones, is allowed to graze naturally, and quite often comes from wild sources, so that the level of omega-3's is higher, levels of saturated fats lower.

Protein Q&A

Q. Where does whey come from?
A. Whey comes from milk. During the process of turning milk into cheese, the whey protein is separated from the curds.

Q. Why use whey?
A. It contains the perfect combination of amino acids, in just the right concentrations for optimal performance in the body. Both hormonal and cellular responses seem to be greatly enhanced by whey supplementation. If you are trying to increase muscle mass, whey protein is invaluable in building and retaining muscle tissue.

Q. How do I know how much protein I need?
A. Easy – just follow these simple calculations. If you are sedentary you need 0.8g protein per kilogram of bodyweight (0.36g per pound of bodyweight). If you are active, you need 1.4g protein per kilogram of bodyweight (0.64g per pound of bodyweight). So a woman weighing 63kg (140lb) who exercises needs 88.2g of protein per day. A woman weighing 63kg (140lb) who isn't active would be fine on 50.4g of protein per day.

Q. Can I have all my protein in one meal?
A. No, it is best to spread it out over the day, so divide it between your three meals and two snacks. You can do this by having eggs at breakfast, a portion of nuts for your morning snack, some fish at lunchtime, a whey protein shake as an afternoon snack, and finally by including a piece of lean meat in your evening meal.

GOOD PROTEIN CHOICES

- **Micro-filtered whey-protein powder**
- **Fish and shellfish**
  Trout, sardines, mackerel, fresh tuna, cod – all of which are rich in omega-3 fatty acids. Bass, sole, herring, tinned tuna, dory, haddock, halibut, snapper, swordfish, green-lipped mussels, squid, oysters, clams, crayfish, lobster, crab, scallops, prawns.
- **Poultry and game**
  Organic or free-range chicken, turkey, wild duck, pheasant, quail, rabbit, venison, wild boar
- **Meats**
  Organic beef, pork, lamb; lean bacon and ham.
- **Eggs**
  Free-range, organic
- **Cheese (maximum 100g/3½oz as an occasional portion)**
  Parmesan, Camembert, feta, cottage, ricotta
- **Soya**
  Tofu (bean curd), tempeh and other soya products with a low carbohydrate content

POOR PROTEIN CHOICES

- Streaky bacon, sausages, salami, processed meat products, fish fingers, battered fish, fishcakes, crabsticks, chicken nuggets

Essential fats

If you have been doggedly avoiding fat in an attempt to lose weight – this approach is WRONG. You need fats in your diet. Your brain consists mostly of fat, and your intelligence, heartbeat and muscular movements all depend on it. The only way in which your body can send electrical messages through living tissue is via your nerve cells and their connectors, which again are made of fat.

The fact is that some fats (known as lipids) are essential. They act as the second energy reserve behind glycogen, providing most of their energy at around 70 per cent of maximum heart rate. Endurance athletes utilize fat as an energy source more than other sports people and this is why they tend to be lean.

Fats are not just for energy, though. Their many other functions include insulating important organs, carrying fat-soluble vitamins and regulating hormone levels. If you're a female athlete and you experience a loss of your periods, this may be due to extremely low body fat, for this plays a vital role in the activation of the female hormone oestrogen.

Fats also contribute to health in many other ways – provided they are of the right kind. In an attempt to warn people about the risk of consuming too much fat, certain groups have created the impression that all fats are bad, but this simply is not true.

Are you eating the wrong fats?

Many people in the Western world are getting 45 per cent of their calorific intake from fats, but these are junk fats that the body cannot use, so these people are just as fat-deficient as those on extremely low-fat regimes.

THERE ARE TWO MAIN TYPES OF NATURAL FATS:
1. Saturated fats come primarily from animal sources such as meat and dairy products, and from coconut and palm-kernel oil; they are solid at room temperature. They provide the body with a stored form of energy in fat cells.
2. Unsaturated fats are found in vegetables, nuts, grains and seeds, and in fish and game; they are liquid at room temperature. They contain two fatty acids that are essential to life and, more importantly, that the body cannot produce itself. These are linoleic acid (omega-6) and linolenic acid (omega-3) From these two 'essential fatty acids' your body can make all the other fatty acids it needs.

THE GOOD

Unrefined vegetable oil (flaxseed oil, olive oil) and fish oil, which are full of omega-3 fatty acids – eat more, more, more.

THE BAD

Large amounts of saturated fats – keep them limited.

AND THE UGLY

Refined, junk fats that are full of hydrogenated/trans fats – show them the door.

Is it just a case of cutting out saturated fat?

Saturated fat gets a bad press, and a diet too heavy in it has been closely linked to cardiovascular disease. However, there is another fat with an equal capacity to harm: hydrogenated fat.

Hydrogenated fat is solid or semi-solid at room temperature (the best example being margarine). It is created when a liquid oil (such as corn oil) has hydrogen added to it, changing its chemical structure. This in turn can interfere with the metabolism of some essential fatty acids. Research has shown that the trans fats in hydrogenated fats can increase LDL (poor) cholesterol, decrease HDL (good) cholesterol and thus raise the risk of coronary heart disease. Hydrogenated fat is found in almost all processed foods, plus frozen convenience foods and deep-fried fast food. This is another good reason to say goodbye to junk food and hello to fresh produce.

If you usually ingest high amounts of processed fats and use commercially altered oils for cooking, then you are certainly not getting the balance of fats that your body needs.

Natural cold-pressed oils and oily fish are vital to maintain good health. They contain essential fatty acids that, amongst other things, boost brain power.

Why don't food manufacturers use healthier oils?

Even though the food industry uses vegetable oils that contain a reasonable amount of omega-6 fatty acids, they avoid omega-3s because these are more susceptible to oxidization – in other words, they go rancid quickly and don't have a long shelf life.

Ironic, isn't it? Food manufacturers quite happily promote food under the guise of lowering cholesterol and reducing heart disease, but they are ignoring one of the fats essential to health. So unless you are eating high amounts of fish, fish oils, leafy vegetables, nuts, unrefined olive oil, tofu or flaxseed oil, your ratio of omega-6 to omega-3 fats is probably screwed up, and this in turn will be screwing up your health.

The current Western diet is much higher in omega-6 fatty acids than omega-3's. Remember those healthy Palaeolithic people we were discussing earlier (see page 14)? They were eating equal amounts of both.

How is this relevant to body weight?

If you are eating a diet with a good balance of omega-6 and omega-3 fatty acids, this will affect your body in beneficial fat-burning ways:

◆ Your metabolic rate will be increased, as will the metabolism of fats, so more stored fat will be burned for energy

GREAT SOURCES OF OMEGA-3
ESSENTIAL FATTY ACIDS

Flaxseed oil

Salmon

Herring

Trout

Sardines

Tuna

Mackerel

Shellfish

Soyabeans

Walnuts

Wheatgerm

GREAT SOURCES OF OMEGA-6
ESSENTIAL FATTY ACIDS

Sunflower oil

Safflower oil

Corn oil

Sesame oil

Soybeans

Egg yolk

Red meats

Evening primrose oil

Borage oil

Blackcurrant oil

Store flaxseeds in an airtight container in the fridge as this rich souce of omega-3s can go rancid very quickly. Grind before use and sprinkle over food or into drinks for an extra nutritional punch.

Oils are best if you drizzle them over food after cooking, as heat destroys their molecular structure and therefore their nutritional value.

◆ Your cells' sensitivity to insulin will be increased, so that it regulates blood-sugar levels more effectively

◆ The ratio of insulin to glucagons will improve, which will unlock the fat-storage banks and again allow fat to be burned as energy

◆ Natural appetite suppressants will kick in.

So if you want to improve your chances of losing weight, you need to up your intake of omega-3 and other healthy fats.

Essential fats Q&A

Q. How often should I eat oily fish per week if I want to consume enough omega-3 fatty acids?

A. You should aim to eat oily fish a minimum of 2–3 times per week, or ensure you use flaxseed oil regularly on salads to raise your levels. Try to eat fish from as safe a source as possible as many coldwater fish are contaminated with heavy metals and pesticides.

Q. How can I avoid hydrogenated fat?

A. Cut out processed food and only use cold-pressed un-refined oils such as olive oil, or coconut oil for cooking. Don't eat fast food that has been deep-fried and avoid butter type spreads. If you did this, then you should be able to avoid consuming dangerous trans fatty acids.

FAT FACTS

According to the American Heart Association (AHA), the introduction of more than 5,000 low-fat and non-fat foods over the past decade has contributed to an obesity epidemic in America:

'The trouble comes when people think they can eat unlimited amounts of reduced-fat cookies, frozen yogurt and cakes. While these foods contain less fat than their full-fat versions, they tend to have more sugar and can be even higher in calories.'

The AHA recommends avoiding excessive amounts of fat substitutes such as olestra, which is found primarily in snack foods. Olestra passes through the body unabsorbed and can cause digestive problems.

The value of exercise

When was the last time you had a good 30–45 minute walk? How many times have you opted to take the car or jumped on a bus to cover a distance that you are quite capable of walking in 20 minutes?

Okay, it's the time factor – the world we live in moves at such a fast pace that we always seem to be chasing our tails. But exercise is vital. You might eat the healthiest diet in the world, take nutritional supplements, avoid alcohol and lay off the cigarettes, but your overall health will not be complete without physical activity.

The basic fact remains that in order to lose weight, less energy should be taken in than is expended. Even someone with a sluggish basal metabolic rate (BMR) – the rate at which we use up energy – can increase it by engaging in regular physical activity.

Exercise more, eat more

The trouble is that many of us view exercise as a chore. We dread it – even hate it. Time to change all that, because to lose fat you must partake in sustained, regular exercise.

The benefit of exercising is that as you lose fat and start to build muscle, you actually burn calories more effectively. Which brings us to the real bonus of all this physical exertion: *the more you exercise, the more you can eat*. The key factor in this equation is good old oxygen. The more oxygen your muscles is supplied with via the red blood cells, the more

Cycling at a medium pace can burn up 210 kilocalories per hour.

effectively they perform their calorie-burning role. A diet that is high in carbohydrates and fats will cause the red blood cells to clump together, slowing down the supply of oxygen and consequently making you function less efficiently.

Metabolism Q&A

Q. What is metabolism?

A. Metabolism is the rate at which your body burns energy. It varies from person to person – you may have a faster or slower metabolism than is normal for a person of your size and weight.

Q. What is basal metabolic rate (BMR)?

A. It is the rate at which you use up energy when you are sleeping or resting.

Q. What is the average person's BMR?

A. As a rough guide, the average BMR is about half a calorie per pound of body weight, per hour. So if you weigh 140lb (63kg), you will use up approximately 70 calories an hour, or 1,680 calories per day if you are doing absolutely nothing.

Q. What makes someone's BMR naturally higher than average?

A. The more you weigh, the higher your BMR will be, but it drops by about 2 per cent per decade, after the age of 20. People whose bodies contain a higher proportion of muscle to fat tend to have a higher BMR than those with lower muscle mass.

Q. Does a high BMR mean it is easier to lose weight?

A. All things being equal, the more energy you need to tick over, the more food you can eat without gaining weight. From that perspective, a high BMR should make it easier to lose weight.

Q. Does your BMR decrease when you start to follow a low-calorie diet?

A. Yes, because in response to fewer calories, your body lowers its BMR, thinking there is a famine. It literally slows down to conserve energy. This is why so many people hit a 'plateau' during dieting.

Q. Can a low BMR cause obesity?

A. Except in cases of rare metabolic illness, it not possible to blame obesity on your metabolism.

Monitoring your heart rate during exercise is important to ensure your level of activity is kept to a desirable pace. It also allows you to monitor progress.

Aerobic exercise

Two types of exercise are necessary to build this new lean body of yours: aerobic exercise and resistance/weight training. Aerobic exercise elevates the heartbeat and requires additional oxygen intake. It includes:

◆ Cycling
◆ Running
◆ Dancing
◆ Trampolining
◆ Skiing
◆ Swimming
◆ Brisk walking
◆ Aerobic classes.

The most important thing is to pick an activity that you enjoy. Either opt for one type of exercise that you know you will do regularly, without the usual excuses, or go for a bit of variety to keep it interesting. Just make sure you do some form of aerobic exercise for 30–45 minutes three or more times per week.

TOP TIPS

Make time each day for some form of physical activity, however slight: take the stairs at work, walk up or down the escalator, or park at the far end of the car park instead of cruising around for the closest spot.

Exercise can be as 'social' or as 'solo' as you want it. If the idea of joining a gym doesn't appeal, take to the streets and run or go for long walks in the country – just get active!

A stronger body burns more calories. Increase your lean body ratio by adding weight training to your exercise regime.

CALORIE-BURNING ACTIVITIES

Even the most mundane tasks can burn off calories, so next time you are faced with a mountain of ironing, enjoy – you are burning off 252 calories per hour!

Activity	Calories expended per hour
Bedmaking	234
Bowling	264
Cleaning windows	350
Cycling (8.8km/h/5½mph)	210
Dancing	330
Desk work	132
Football	450
Gardening	250
General housework	190
Golf	300
Horse riding	480
Ironing	252
Jogging	500
Mowing the lawn	462
Running	900
Skiing	594
Swimming	500
Walking (4km/h/2½mph)	116

Resistance/weight training

Resistance training helps boost energy levels, burn fat and strengthen the joints; improves posture and bone density; stimulates the elimination of waste via the lymphatic system, thereby reducing cellulite; and increases levels of the rejuvenating growth hormone. Forms of resistance training include:

◆ Free weights: either use weights attached to your wrists and ankles or straightforward dumbbells

◆ Weight machines: these specialist gym machines exercise different muscle groups; it is important to work with an instructor because every machine varies and needs to be geared to your specific requirements

◆ Rubber bands and tubes: these come in a variety of colours denoting their level of resistance; they are highly effective and are brilliant for use at home or when travelling

◆ Gravity resistance: including push-ups, lunges, squats and sit-ups, which build muscle because you are working against gravity to increase strength

◆ Water workouts: a very gentle form of resistance training, ideal for anyone with muscular or skeletal problems.

After one 60-minute session of weight or resistance training, your metabolism continues to burn fat for 24 hours. How about that for an incentive? You should be aiming to do three to four sessions per week. You may find that as your muscles begin to develop, you see a shift upwards on the weighing scales – but don't panic. Dense muscle tissue weighs more than fat, and you should judge your progress by the way your clothes fit, not by your weight.

CAUTION

Before you start any exercise regime, check your overall fitness with your doctor or with a qualified gym instructor.

Diet

Low-carb lifestyle guidelines

By now you should have a pretty clear idea of what you have to do to improve your diet and, with it, your entire lifestyle.

The general principles

- Cut out all unhealthy refined carbohydrates (see page 18).
- Curb your intake of high GI carbohydrates and focus on those from the low–medium GI range (see page 21).
- Eat most of your fruit and vegetables raw to ensure a good level of phytonutrients (see page 22) and fibre.
- Eat more high-quality protein (see page 29) – organic if at all possible.
- Increase your intake of healthy omega-3 fatty acids (see page 32) by eating more oily fish, and use only natural unrefined oils in your cooking.
- Cut out tea, coffee, concentrated fruit juices and alcohol, and banish soft drinks of any kind, but drink at least eight glasses of water per day.
- Incorporate 30–45 minutes of aerobic exercise (see page 36) at least three times in to your weekly routine, and carry out resistance training (see page 37) at least three times per week.

Colourful salads should be an essential part of your daily diet.

Are you all fired up?

You should be, because you are going to get back in control. You now know what you are doing, understand your body and should look on this as an important project that will bring untold benefits. Now that you understand how your body metabolizes the food that you eat, you can start to view food as a vital fuel that helps your body function at optimum levels. This should be a turning point. It should change your attitude from one of 'Oh no, I'm on a diet' to a more positive 'I'm doing this for me, to make myself healthier, fitter, stronger, leaner'.

Pretty soon you are going to be feeling and looking better. Think of that boost of self-confidence that you are going to experience. So get ready to roll and flex that determination. Whether you have 3kg (7lb) to lose or 30kg (70lb), this regime is only going to work if you are committed to changing your eating and exercise habits for life.

The rest of this section offers advice on weight, and on setting goals for (and managing) weight loss; suggests how to cope with the cravings and snack attacks that may arise when you are on a diet; and gives tips on taking supplements and sticking to a healthy diet, even when you lead a busy lifestyle. It is followed by the three-step programme and nutritious recipes that form the mainstay of this book. Plus, there is also a section on adapting the plans to suit a vegetarian diet, which includes some delicious low-carb vegetarian recipes.

Case Study

I am the dieter from hell and I've been yo-yo dieting for over 25 years. I have tried to eat healthily, but my bad habits keep creeping back in, and I have always eaten a diet that is quite high in carbohydrates.

Breakfast would usually be soaked oats with nuts, seeds and raisins or toast and marmalade, some fruit and several cups of coffee. Lunch would be a baked potato or pasta. My husband cooks in the evening, and he's a fabulous cook, so I always eat too much and usually drink a few glasses of wine as well. I don't have a particularly sweet tooth, so that's not my problem, but I have a small (3-year-old) boy and I tend to eat whatever he doesn't want.

This regime (don't think of it as a diet) really does hold out hope for me. It's the easiest and most pleasant diet I've ever been on. I didn't feel hungry and the meals (I followed the Fast Track plan for two weeks) were delicious. Best of all, I had incredible energy for the entire time and I felt lighter and much less bloated than usual. I lost 1.8kg (4 lb) the first week, which I was really happy about as my body hangs onto weight like nothing on earth, after two weeks I was 3.2 kg (7lb) lighter.

I am sticking to the ground rules, and have only broken them once, but I felt so shattered and bloated after eating an illicit piece of cake and a slice of toast, that I have learned my lesson.

Basically, I'm beyond impressed. Diets simply haven't worked for me before – and I'm talking about almost 30 years of dieting!

Jane Tierney Jones 42, writer and mother

The weight question

'Those desiring to lose weight should perform hard work before food. They should take their meals after exertion and while still panting from fatigue . . . They should, moreover, eat only once a day and take no baths and sleep on a hard bed and walk naked as long as possible.'

Hippocrates (c. 460–377 BC), the father of medicine, on his dieting philosophy

Theories on the weight-loss benefits of walking around naked and not bathing have not been proven, but Hippocrates' other dietary advice isn't completely off the wall and shows that even 2,400 years ago, the relationship between food intake and energy expenditure was recognized.

Today 'obesity' is becoming universally recognized as a disease in its own right. Obese and overweight are terms that are often used interchangeably, but let's clarify the difference between them:

◆ Overweight refers to an excess of body weight and includes all tissues, such as fat, bone and muscle, but not just excess body fat.

◆ Obese means that someone is carrying an excessively high proportion of body fat that could compromise their health.

If you are an athlete or body-builder, you may weigh more than the desirable weight range for your height (see page 124), but this is normal because muscle weighs more than fat. Equally, you may be a relatively sedentary person who weighs in at the correct weight for your height, but who still carries too high a proportion of body fat. In this case, a good exercise programme is vital.

For those of you who feel that you are more 'lard' than 'hard', and don't like what you are seeing on the scales, a better way of calculating just how overweight you are is by working out your Body Mass Index (BMI).

You can tell if you have surplus body fat simply by seeing if you can pinch more than 2.5cm (1in) on your hips, tummy, underarms and back.

CALCULATING YOUR BMI

In 1997 a WHO convention agreed on an international standard for measuring overweight and obesity – the Body Mass Index (BMI), defined as weight (in kilograms) divided by the square of your height (in metres): kg/m2.

To obtain your BMI, use one of the following methods:

1. **Divide your weight in kilograms by your height in metres squared.**
2. **Multiply your weight in pounds by 700; divide the result by your height in inches, then divide it a second time by your height in inches.**
3. **Search on the internet for an interactive BMI calculator.**

Results

Underweight	= under BMI 20kg/m2
Average weight	= BMI 20–25kg/m2
Overweight	= BMI 25kg/m2
Pre-obese	= BMI 25–29.9 kg/m2
Class I obese	= 30–34.9 kg/m2
Class II obese	= BMI 35–39.9 kg/m2
Class III obese	= BMI 40 kg/m2

your **weight**	your **height**	your **BMI**

Alternatively, get your doctor or gym instructor to check out your BMI using callipers, or buy a set yourself from your local pharmacy. If you have more than 25 per cent body fat, then the chances are that you are carrying too much weight, or at the very least need to change your diet and participate in exercise that will burn fat and build muscle.

Successful weight loss and healthy weight management depend on sensible goals and expectations – losing just 5–10 per cent of your weight is the kind of goal that can help improve your health.

You may be wondering how you have got this far into the book without hearing about calories. But you don't need to become obsessed with the calorific value of everything you put in your mouth. Instead, it is much better to check food labels to see if the food contains unnecessary additives, sugar, hydrogenated fats and salt – and, of course, how high the carbohydrate content is.

Take a health check . . .

Before you begin a new dietary regime or exercise programme, check with your doctor that your health status allows you to do so. A health check is vital if:

◆ You are suffering from any ongoing health problems
◆ You take regular medication
◆ You are under 20 or over 65, because children, teenagers and the elderly have specific nutritional needs.

And a reality check ...

◆ If you do have a problem with your weight, stop beating yourself up over it. Being fat is not a sin or a criminal offence. It is simply a consequence of careless eating and lifestyle.
◆ Even if you have tried every diet going, this one does not have to be the same. You are going to change your lifestyle and give up a few bad dietary habits. So, unless you have a medical condition that prevents you from losing weight, this approach will help you become slimmer and, more importantly, fitter.
◆ Being overweight can undermine your self-esteem and the way you deal with situations. Losing weight won't change the fact that you have money worries, an unsupportive partner or hate your job, but when the pounds start to fall away and you begin to feel better about yourself, you will deal with those issues very differently. Your confidence levels will rise and you will have lots more energy, which will help to make all of your problems seem more manageable.
◆ Don't be negative even before you start. This is not the problem you think it is – it's the solution.

OBESITY AS A DISEASE – NOT A MORAL FAILING

According to a 1995 report from the US Institute of Medicine,

'Obesity is a heterogeneous disease in which genetic, environmental, psychological, and other factors are involved. It occurs when energy intake exceeds the amount of energy expended over time. Only in a small minority of cases is obesity caused by such illnesses as hypothyroidism or the result of taking medications, such as steroids, that can cause weight gain.'

TAKING A HOLISTIC APPROACH

What you weigh is the result of several factors:

◆ **How much and what kinds of food you eat**
◆ **Whether your lifestyle includes regular physical activity**
◆ **Whether you use food to respond to stress and other situations**
◆ **Your physiological and genetic make-up**
◆ **Your age and health status.**

Successful weight management should address all of these factors. That's the reason for ignoring products that promise quick and easy solutions, or permanent results without permanent changes in lifestyle. Any product that promises that you can lose weight without lowering your calorie intake and/or increasing your physical activity is trading on fantasy and false hope.

Monitoring weight loss

There are two schools of thought on how to monitor weight loss:

◆ Daily weighing

◆ The once-weekly weigh-in.

This is an individual issue. If you are the sort of person who needs a daily date with your weighing scales, then by all means do so. Keep a record of your progress using a chart like the one opposite. You may see weight-shifting patterns emerging and be able to isolate foods that have a negative effect on your weight. If you prefer the surprise-at-the-end-of-the-week, that is fine too. You should still keep a record and watch out for any plateaux where weight loss dries up, which may mean that you need to lower your carbohydrate levels or increase your physical activity.

Whichever your preferred monitoring method, keep a tight-fitting pair of trousers or other item of clothing and try them on regularly to establish how your shape is changing. Your weight may stabilize for a while, and if you are exercising regularly and increasing your muscle-to-fat ratio you may even may weigh slightly more for a bit, but you will be fitter and – in the end – leaner.

Don't become obsessed with the scales –
judge your progress by taking notice of how
your clothes are fitting you.

TOP ANTI-SNACKING TIPS

◆ **Try not to snack while watching television, playing video games or using the computer. Eat meals and snacks in the kitchen or dining room, so that you are more aware of what – and how much – you are eating.**

◆ **When you feel a snack attack coming on, run a bath, go for a walk, ring a friend… Do anything that will keep you away from the refrigerator.**

◆ **Don't go shopping when you are hungry – it is then that you may reach out for that chocolate bar.**

◆ **If you are going to snack, make sure it is a protein snack.**

Dietary demons – and how to beat them

1. **Not so well-meaning friends and family members:** one of the most difficult things to deal with is the friend or relative who tries to sway you off-course. Don't be bullied into breaking your resolve. Decline politely and explain that you are relying on them for support. If you are visiting them, take a whey-protein smoothie with you.

2. **Boredom:** you shouldn't get bored following the plans in this book, because there are so many different things to eat and ways to prepare your food. Even if you aren't a natural cook, experimenting in the kitchen will keep you motivated.

3. **Alcohol:** you are allowed a couple of glasses of wine when you start the Keep on Tracking Plan, but don't be tempted to have more. There is nothing like a little extra alcohol to persuade you that you'll start again tomorrow. Avoid the 'drunken munchies'.

4. **Snack attacks:** the three dietary plans allow for a couple of high-protein snacks each day between meals, but you could easily undermine all your efforts by hitting the biscuit jar in a moment of weakness. Clear out anything vaguely tempting from your refrigerator and cupboards, and be very careful at times when you normally seek comfort food.

Curb your cravings by curbing your carbs

When you start eating more healthily and reducing the amount of potentially addictive carbohydrate-laden foods, you should find that your cravings begin to diminish as your blood-sugar and insulin levels even out. This will usually take about 48 hours when you start the Fast-Track Plan (see page 58). If you do get a 'snack attack', try making yourself a whey-protein smoothie; or keep a plate of cold chicken in the refrigerator for weak moments. You can't necessarily kill a craving, but you can wrestle it into submission.

	day 1	day 2	day 3	day 4	day 5	day 6	day 7	total
week 1								
week 2								
week 3								

Taking pills and supplements

Pills and supplements both have their uses, but only in moderation and only as long as strict guidelines are followed.

Over-the-counter (OTC) diet pills

The 1991/2 Weight Loss Practices Survey, sponsored by the US Food and Drug Administration (FDA) and the National Heart, Lung and Blood Institute, found that 5 per cent of women and 2 per cent of men trying to lose weight use diet pills. Products considered by the FDA to be OTC weight-control drugs are primarily those containing the active ingredient phenylpropanolamine (PPA), such as Dexatrim and Acutrim. PPA is available over the counter for weight control in a 75mg controlled-release-dosage form. The medicine should be used in combination with a restricted diet and exercise.

Using diet pills containing PPA will not make a big difference in the rate of weight loss, says Robert Sherman of the FDA's Office of OTC Drug Evaluation. 'Even the best studies show only about a half pound (250g) greater weight loss per week using PPA combined with diet and exercise,' he adds. Sherman

In the UK alone, 300 million pounds is spent on diet pills and supplements each year.

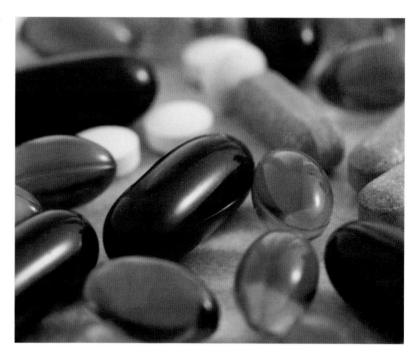

Key supplements

Magnesium	A fundamentally important mineral that counters insulin resistance. It is hugely deficient in the Western diet. Consider taking 230–600mg per day, unless you have suffered kidney failure or have a high degree of AV heart block.
Quercetin	A flavonoid with powerful anti-inflammatory properties that helps to control high insulin levels and inhibit fat production. Take 200–400mg three times a day before meals.
Omega-3 fats	If you don't eat fish, take 1,000–3,000mg of fish oil daily in capsule form. Vegetarians can use flaxseed oil or crushed flaxseeds instead of fish oil capsules. Try flaxseed oil in salad dressings (or even in smoothies) to ensure you get enough of this health-enhancing fat.
Chromium	A trace element that plays an important role in carbohydrate metabolism and regulating blood-sugar levels. It has proved useful in treating diabetes and shown to be effective in encouraging the body to lose fat, not muscle, when dieting. Take 400–600mcg of chromium picolinate or chromiumpolynicotinate a day.
L-carnitine	Used extensively by athletes to ensure maximum performance in endurance or aerobic sports. It is also useful for weight loss because it is involved in burning fat in muscle cells. Take 1,000–3,000mg per day.

cautions that the recommended dosage of these pills should not be exceeded because of the risk of possible adverse effects, such as raised blood pressure and heart palpitations.

Supplements

To rely on taking pills as a way of supplying nutrients is not ideal, for in a perfect world such nutrients should come from our food. But when you consider the quality of some of our food – fruit and vegetables grown in mineral-depleted soil, picked before they have ripened and shipped over vast distances in refrigeration, then put into long-term storage; meat full of hormones; grains stripped of most of their nutritional content – then taking a good multivitamin supplement and possibly extra vitamin C can benefit most people. And while you are trying to balance your blood-sugar levels, reduce body fat and rebuild lean muscle tissue, there are a few supplements that may help.

The 3-step programme

The dietary plans that follow offer simple, nutritious and delicious recipes on a staged regime that should take you from overweight to optimum weight and enhanced well-being.

The reason many people depend on junk and convenience foods is because they lead such busy lives. Most of the recipes in these plans are quick to prepare, and should be within the capabilities of even the most reluctant cook. There are exceptions: preparing the Chicken Soup on page 67 will take a couple of hours, but it makes a lot and you can freeze separate portions, ensuring that you can have a nutritious low-carb meal even when the clock is ticking away.

So blitz your cupboards and discard any foodstuffs that don't fit the bill. The journey to a healthy, lean body begins here.

The Plans

The 3–step programme includes 3 eating plans. The Fast-Track Plan will help you lose weight quickly and give you that all-important boost on a 50 per cent protein/20 per cent carbohydrate/30 per cent fat regime that will initiate benign dietary ketosis (see page 52). It should last for 7–21 days, after which you are ready to move on to the next stage. Your weight loss should be around 2–5.5kg (4–12lb) if you are a woman and 4–7.25kg (8–16lb) if you are a man, depending on how long you remain on this plan.

During the Keep on Tracking Plan you increase your levels of low-to-medium GI carbohydrates and move into a 35 per cent protein/35 per cent carbohydrate/30 per cent fat regime. You still monitor ketosis and watch how introducing higher levels of carbohydrates affects your weight loss, which should now even out to 0.25–1kg (½–2lb) per week.

The No Backtracking Plan is your eating regime for life. You can gradually introduce fruit and vegetables, grains and pulses from the higher GI ranges, in moderation. It is important to keep an eye on how your body reacts to these and to establish your perfect weight-management level.

If you are a vegetarian, there is plenty of advice on how to adapt the plans and recipes to suit your dietary requirements (see pages 106–119). Granted, your choice isn't as varied as that of a non-vegetarian, but don't use this as an excuse not to give it a go. If you follow the basic guidelines and make simple changes to the recipes where necessary, you should lose weight and eradicate insulin resistance successfully.

FOOD TO THROW OUT

- ◆ **White flour and sugar**
- ◆ **Honey**
- ◆ **Biscuits**
- ◆ **Crisps**
- ◆ **Sweets**
- ◆ **Sugary drinks**
- ◆ **White rice, bread, pasta**
- ◆ **Processed foods high in carbohydrates**
- ◆ **Ready-made sauces**
- ◆ **Gravy mixes**

The key to sticking to a diet is to keep your food as interesting and varied as possible.

Customize the plans to suit your lifestyle and dietary preferences

The suggested menu plans are not set in stone – they are templates to encourage you to eat the right sort and amount of food.

If you wish to change a recipe – because you don't like lamb and would rather have chicken, say – it really doesn't matter. Just try to use foods of a similar dietary value. When swapping vegetables and fruit, go for ones in the same GI category; try to exchange meat for meat, or fish for fish, in the same amounts. If you change a recipe from meat to fish, you may need to use slightly more fish to give you the same level of protein. For example, 125g (4oz) of poultry or lean meat should be replaced with 175g (6oz) of fish. Check the tables on pages 56 to establish the protein values of various foods, then adjust accordingly.

Simplify the recipes

If you are short of time, or like your food a bit plainer, simplify the recipe. If you don't fancy Baked Tuna with Tomato and Herbs, adapt the ingredients, ensuring that you still have sufficient protein, carbohydrates and healthy fats – have a tuna salad with tomatoes and dark green leaves.

On a budget

If money is short and you find some of the suggested ingredients a little expensive, use some budgetary ingenuity to bring down the cost. Fresh salmon can be replaced with coley or whiting, or even tinned salmon.

Use the suggested meals as inspiration. In order to manage your weight in the future, you will have to experiment and be prepared to adapt.

TheP

lans

Fast-Track

Fast-Track principles

This is a diet, or a way of eating, that will:

◆ Lower insulin levels and stabilize blood-sugar levels
◆ Banish food cravings
◆ Eliminate energy peaks and troughs, and mood swings
◆ Enhance concentration
◆ Re-educate you into a way of eating that will increase your vitality and improve your overall health
◆ Help your body to burn fat and normalize your weight.

It is vital that you understand the principles of this diet and follow it responsibly. If you are fundamentally healthy, but insulin-resistant and experiencing any of the accompanying symptoms (see page 17), this plan will help you redress the balance and find a level of carbohydrate intake with which your system can cope. The Fast-Track Plan offers you a kick-start and is aimed at women with a BMI of over 35 and men with a BMI of over 25 (see page 42).

For the period of this plan you base your diet on an approximate ratio of 50 per cent high-quality protein/20 per cent low GI carbohydrates/30 per cent healthy fats. You begin the first two weeks of the diet by restricting your carbohydrate intake to 20g (¾oz), your protein to 150g (5oz) Biological Value and healthy fats to a minimum of 40g (1½oz). On a very simplistic level this means:

◆ 3 cups low GI vegetables per day.
◆ 1½ portions of protein three times per day and ½ portion twice per day as a snack. (A portion of protein is the equivalent to the size of your palm.)
◆ Around a half to a whole teaspoon of allowable fats at every meal.

Within 48 hours your body will start to burn its own fat as fuel, as your body switches into benign dietary ketosis.

Ketosis

Being in ketosis means that your body burns fat because it isn't taking in sufficient glucose to meet your energy needs. Under everyday conditions the carbohydrates that you eat are converted to glucose, which is the body's primary source of energy. Whenever your carbohydrate intake is limited to a certain range, for a long enough period of time, your body will draw on its fat stores – turning this into a source of fuel called ketones. When you burn a

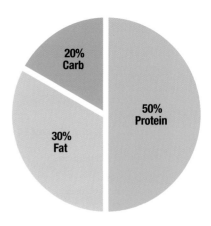

Reducing carbohydrates to a minimum in the initial phase will help kick start your system.

Case Study

For a couple of comfort food addicts, this wasn't the easiest regime to follow. We both love chocolates and sweets (particularly Jim!) and can't pass up any form of pudding. We also tend to entertain a lot, which involves cooking, and we really don't hold back on the rich sauces and bread. We regularly diet, but we never seem to find the time for exercise because we have two small children. Whatever approach we try, we tend to give up and go back to our usual habits after a few days.

The first couple of days on this diet were a complete nightmare – we were hungry all the time. Jim caved in and had a couple of biscuits (out of sheer starvation) on the first night. But it got better by the third day, particularly when we realised that we could have cooked breakfasts. Best of all was the fact that we started losing weight really quickly. We both lost 2.7kg (6lb) within the first four days and in total Joanna lost 4kg (9lb) and Jim lost 5.4kg (12lb) in two weeks.

The diet certainly became easier as we continued. We found it pretty tough not eating the carbohydrates that we love – and in particular avoiding chocolate or coffee – but we have noticed that we are craving those foods less and less. Hopefully we will be able to manage our weight by eating those things as treats, rather than the staple part of our diet, in the future.

Joanna (34) and Jim (35) Cartwright – she's an accountant and he's an IT consultant.

larger amount of fat than is immediately needed for energy, the excess ketones are discarded in the urine.

Dietary ketosis has received a bad press because it is often confused with ketoacidosis, a life-threatening condition most often associated with insulin-deficient, type 1 diabetes.

Benign dietary ketosis, however, is a natural adjustment to the body's reduced intake of carbohydrates, as the body shifts its primary source of energy from carbohydrates to stored fat. The presence of insulin keeps ketone production in check so that a mild beneficial ketosis is achieved. Blood-sugar levels are stabilized within a normal range and there is no breakdown of healthy muscle tissue, as long as sufficient protein is included in the diet.

Measuring ketosis

On a rapid weight-loss diet you will usually start to burn fat instead of sugar within the first 48 hours. To measure the ketone levels in your urine, buy urinary test strips, called lypolisis strips, from any pharmacy, which will show you if your carbohydrate/insulin balance is at optimum levels for fat burning. You should do this twice a day: before breakfast and before your evening meal. Your levels need to be between trace and small (0.5–1.5 mmol-l).

Caution: if your levels rise to above moderate (4 mmol-l), you are not eating enough and should increase your low GI carbohydrates until the ketones are reduced to between trace and small (0.5–1.5 mmol-l). Always drink plenty of water: at least eight large glasses per day.

Fast-Track rules

During this first two weeks you need to:

◆ Eat about 150g (5oz) of protein per day, which should come from a portion about the size of your palm at each meal, plus two all-protein snacks per day (see page 56).

◆ Eat around 20g of carbohydrates per day. A simple way to work this out is to use a set of measuring cups (a cup holds 250ml/8 fl oz). You should aim to eat approximately 3 cups of low GI vegetables or 2 cups of low GI vegetables and ½ cup low GI fruit – at least half of which should be eaten raw. See the Quick Carb Guide on page 56 for a list of low GI vegetables and fruit.

◆ Get 30 per cent of your daily calorific intake from fats, which may include: olive oil, walnut oil, grapeseed oil, coconut oil, homemade mayonnaise, flaxseed oil, small amounts of butter, small amounts of sour cream

◆ Drink 8–10 glasses of water daily; you can also drink herbal teas, but avoid alcohol, soft drinks, tea and coffee, because caffeine interferes with ketosis

◆ Avoid artificial sweeteners, which can stimulate insulin secretion

◆ Rev up your protein levels by including at least one whey-protein drink per day

◆ Eat enough – otherwise you may start to burn muscle tissue

◆ Avoid starchy, carbohydrate-heavy foods such as pasta, bread and potatoes

◆ Beware of hidden carbohydrates in sauces and dressings

◆ Check the labels of all foodstuffs and avoid all processed foods

◆ Not give up!

Dietary Q&A

Q. I have been restricting my carbohydrate intake for days now and I have no energy. I thought this plan was supposed to make me feel better, not worse.

A. Your body is adapting to the metabolic conversion of burning fat for energy instead of glucose. This takes about three days in most people, which is why it is usually best to start the diet over a weekend when you are able to relax more. After three days you should see a rise in your energy levels, but if you continue to feel lethargic or unwell, stop the plan and check with your doctor.

Q. Will I get enough fibre on this plan?

A. Fibre is provided by the inclusion of fibrous vegetables and fruit, and is increased if you eat most of these raw. However, if you experience constipation during the initial stages, try adding psyllium husks or psyllium-husk powder to your whey smoothies, because they comprise 100 per cent soluble fibre. Psyllium husks are pure dietary fibre, composed mostly of cellulose. They swell when they come into contact with water and release a gelatinous mass (mucilage) which passes through the colon and aids easy elimination.

Q. Why does a low-carbohydrate diet cause bad breath?

A. When you are on the Fast-Track Plan and restricting your carbohydrates to around 20g (¾oz) per day, you will be burning ketones, which may cause your breath to smell a little unpleasant. Don't worry, this is easily masked by chewing parsley-oil capsules or by using a natural breath-freshener spray. Make sure that you drink plenty of water because this will help to neutralize the odour.

At-a-glance guide

These portions contain roughly 5g (¼oz) of carbohydrates.

Dairy

150g (5oz) mozzarella cheese
100g (3½oz) cottage cheese
150g (5oz) ricotta cheese
100g (3½oz) double cream

Fruit

25g (1oz) blueberries
25g (1oz) raspberries
100g (3½oz) strawberries
50g (2oz) cantaloupe or
    honeydew melon

Juices

60ml (2fl oz) lemon juice
60ml (2fl oz) lime juice
125ml (4fl oz) tomato juice

Vegetables

200g (7oz) cups raw or cooked spinach
90g (3oz) red peppers
1 medium tomato
175g (6oz) raw broccoli
8 medium asparagus spears
175g (6oz) cauliflower
50g (2oz) chopped onion
½ avocado
100g (3½oz) summer squash

Nuts and seeds

25g (1oz) macadamias
25g (1oz) walnuts
25g (1oz) almonds
25g (1oz) pecans
25g (1oz) hulled sunflower seeds
25g (1oz) roasted shelled peanuts
15g (½oz) cashews

Quick guides

Quick carb guide

When choosing carbohydrates on the Fast-Track Plan you should include up to 3 cups (see page 54) of the following vegetables (preferably raw) every day:

Low and medium GI vegetables for the Fast-Track Plan		
Alfalfa sprouts	Radishes	Cauliflower
Kale	Aubergine	Green beans
Lettuce	Celery	Onions
Bok choy	Silver beet	Garlic
Spinach	Turnip	Brussels sprouts
Parsley	Asparagus	Courgette
Cabbage	Broccoli	Cucumber
Mushrooms	Red or green pepper	Water chestnuts

If you want some fruit, substitute one of the above portions for ½ cup of the following:

Low and medium GI fruit for the Fast-Track Plan		
Apricots	Raspberries	Grapefruit
Blackberries	Strawberries	Melon

This should ensure that you are consuming approximately 20g (¾oz) of carbohydrates per day, which should initiate dietary ketosis and fat burning.

Quick protein guide

This will give you a general idea of the protein content of foods, based on a 125g (4oz) portion, unless otherwise stated.

Food	Protein
Meat:	
Chicken	30g
Turkey	30g
Duck	25g
Lamb	30g
Beef	25g
Pork	25g
Rabbit	35g
Venison	35g
Ham	23g
Fish:	
Tuna	26g
Salmon	20g
Sardines	28g
Mackerel	21g
Cod	18g
Hake	20g
Monkfish	18g
Prawns	19g
Crab	22g
Scallops	29g
Tofu	9g
Micro-filtered whey protein (28g scoop)	18–20g
Egg (1)	8g

Super snacks

Here are some good ideas for low-carb, high-protein snacks.

Food	Amount	Carbs	Protein	Fat
Hard-boiled egg	1 egg	1g	8g	7g
Tuna, canned in water or brine	50g (2oz)	–	13g	3g
Sardines, canned in water or brine	50g (2oz)	–	12g	5g
Sunflower or pumpkin seeds	25g (1oz)	5g	6.5g	14g
Almonds	25g (1oz)	5g	6g	15g
Hazelnuts	25g (1oz)	4g	4g	17g
Walnuts	25g (1oz)	5g	4g	15g
Macadamia nuts	25g (1oz)	4g	2.2g	21g
Micro-filtered whey-protein smoothie	15g (½oz)	check the label for nutritional details		
Cottage cheese	50g (2oz)	1g	7.7g	2g
Lean chicken	50g (2oz)	–	8g	1.2g
Lean ham slices	50g (2oz)	0.5g	10g	1.8g
Olives	50g (2oz)	–	0.5g	6g

Bad snacks

Compare the super snacks with these high-carbohydrate foods – and fight the temptation.

Food	Amount	Carbs	Protein	Fat
Crisps	100g (3½oz)	49g	5.6g	37g
Chocolate biscuits (2)	25g (1oz)	18g	1.6g	7.7g
Ice cream	125g (4oz)	27g	3.9g	89g
2 Slices of toast	50g (2oz)	32g	5.2g	0.8g
Chocolate Bar	125g (4oz)	64g	9.7g	30g
Boiled sweets	50g (2oz)	49g	–	–
Jam Doughnut	40g (1½oz)	19.5g	5.8g	2.2g
Slice of pizza	70g (3oz)	18g	7.8g	5.4g
Portion of fries	70g (3oz)	24g	2.6g	13g
Muffin	75g (3oz)	37g	3.65g	8.5g
Sausage roll	100g (3½oz)	25g	10g	27g

The Fast-Track Plan

BREAKFAST

Mushroom Omelette
see page 110, use 3 eggs and replace spinach with 40g (1½oz) mushrooms
4g carbs
20g fat
18g protein

Bacon and tomato
40g (1½oz) lean bacon and 1 medium tomato
5g carbs
20g fat
11g protein

Whey Smoothie
see page 60, use 2 scoops of flavoured whey-protein powder
5g carbs
1g fat
40g protein

Scrambled Tofu
see page 60
2.1g carbs
31g fat
22g protein

SNACK

Chicken
100g (3½oz) lean chicken (hot or cold)
0g carbs
2g fat
30g protein

Whey Smoothie
see page 60, use 1 scoop of whey-protein powder
3g carbs
0.5g fat
20g protein

Hard-boiled egg
1g carbs
5.5g fat
6g protein

Whey Smoothie
see page 60, use 1 scoop of micro-filtered whey-protein powder
3g carbs
1g fat
20g protein

LUNCH

Parma Ham, Parmesan and Rocket Salad
125g (4oz) Parma ham, 15g (½oz) Parmesan cheese and 75g (2½oz) rocket
6.5g carbs
18g fat
37g protein

Salad Niçoise
see page 62
7g carbs
36g fat
34.9g protein

Avocado and Prawn Salad with Lime and Passion-Fruit Dressing
see page 61
4.7g carbs
42g fat
26g protein

Salmon Fillet with Anchovy and Rosemary Salsa
see page 69
5g carbs
33g fat
30.4g protein

SNACK

Tuna
50g (2oz) tuna
0g carbs
3g fat
13g protein

Feta cheese
25g (1oz) feta cheese
0g carbs
8g fat
4g protein

Sardines
50g (2oz) sardines
0g carbs
10g fat
12g protein

Ham
50g (2oz) lean ham
0.5g carbs
2g fat
10g protein

DINNER

Pork and Spinach Stir-Fry
see page 63
6g carbs
27g fat
30g protein

Chicken Soup
see page 67
5.6g carbs
25g fat
36g protein

Lamb Chops with Aubergine Salad and Mint Raita
see pages 66 and 67
10g carbs
30g fat
32.5g protein

Thai Prawn Soup
see page 65
9g carbs
30g fat
40g protein

Whey Smoothie see page 60, use 2 scoops of flavoured whey-protein powder **5g carbs** **1g fat** **40g protein**	**Kippers and tomato** 2 kippers and 1 grilled tomato **5g carbs** **10g fat** **20g protein**	**Salmon and scrambled eggs** 2 slices smoked salmon with 2 scrambled eggs **2g carbs** **16g fat** **43g protein**	**BREAKFAST**
Sunflower or pumpkin seeds 25g (1oz) sunflower or pumpkin seeds **5g carbs** **14g fat** **6.5g protein**	**Cottage cheese** 5g (2oz) cottage cheese **1g carbs** **2g fats** **7.7g protein**	**Walnuts** 25g (1oz) walnuts **5g carbs** **15g fat** **4g protein**	**SNACK**
Coleslaw-Plus see page 61 **6g carbs** **25g fat** **10g protein**	**Turkey and Broccoli Salad** see page 63 **10g carbs** **20g fat** **35g protein**	**Beef steak, spinach and green beans** 175g (6oz) lean beef steak, 75g (2½oz) spinach and 75g (2½oz) green beans **8g carbs** **10g fat** **37g protein**	**LUNCH**
Lamb 50g (2oz) lean lamb **0g carbs** **4g fat** **16g protein**	**Macadamia nuts** 25g (1oz) macadamia nuts **4g carbs** **21g fat** **2.2g protein**	**Feta cheese and black olives** 25g (1oz) feta cheese with a couple of black olives **1g carbs** **5g fat** **4.5g protein**	**SNACK**
Baked Tuna with Tomato and Herbs see page 70 **8g carbs** **20g fat** **31g protein**	**Ginger-Poached Cod with Confetti Cabbage** see page 68 **8.5g carbs** **1.5g fat** **32.5g protein**	**Chicken and asparagus with Hollandaise Sauce** 125g (4oz) grilled chicken breast, 125g (4oz) asparagus and hollandaise sauce (see page 120) **5.4g carbs** **63g fat** **42g protein**	**DINNER**

Whey Smoothie with Berries

Serves 1
Carbs 10g
Fat 0.5g
Protein 18g

1. Put the frozen berries, whey-protein powder and ice cubes into a food processor or blender with about 2.5cm/1in of the water and blend for approximately 20 seconds. Add more water if you want a thinner smoothie.

VARIATIONS
To make a plain whey smoothie, simply omit the berries. If you aren't used to the flavour of whey-powder then try adding a little natural vanilla essence.

50g (2 oz) frozen berries, such as raspberries, strawberries, blackberries

25g (1oz) scoop micro-filtered whey-protein powder

3 ice cubes

still mineral water

Scrambled Tofu

Serves 1
Carbs 2.1g
Fat 31g
Protein 22g

1. Heat the oil in a frying pan and sauté the spring onion until soft.
2. Mash the tofu and put it into the pan with the turmeric, curry powder and cumin. Season to taste with salt and pepper and cook on a high heat for about 2–3 minutes, until the tofu is firm. Sprinkle the cheese on top and serve immediately.

1 tablespoon extra virgin olive oil

1 spring onion, finely chopped

200g (7oz) tofu

pinch of turmeric

½ teaspoon curry powder

¼ teaspoon ground cumin

1 tablespoon grated Cheddar or Parmesan cheese

salt and pepper

Avocado and Prawn Salad with Lime and Passion-Fruit Dressing

75g (2½oz) mixed leaves

½ avocado, cubed

100g (3½oz) cooked peeled prawns

1 celery stick, finely chopped

Lime and passion-fruit dressing

1 tablespoon olive or flaxseed oil

1 teaspoon walnut oil

juice of ½ lime

juice and seeds of 1 passion fruit

½ small red chilli, deseeded and finely chopped (optional)

salt and pepper

Serves 1
Carbs 4.7g
Fat 42g
Protein 25.8g

1. First make the dressing. Blend the olive or flaxseed oil, walnut oil, lime juice, passion-fruit juice and seeds and chilli with salt and pepper until smooth, then taste and adjust the seasoning as necessary.
2. Arrange the mixed leaves on a plate. Gently combine the avocado, prawns and celery with the dressing, pile on to the leaves and serve.

Coleslaw-Plus

Serves 2
Carbs 6g
Fat 25g
Protein 10g

1. Put the shredded green and red cabbage, celery, red pepper, spring onion, grated cheese, poppy seeds, sesame seeds and bouillon powder in a bowl then mix together. Stir in the mayonnaise. If you like a sharper taste, add a squeeze of fresh lemon juice.

50g (2oz) shredded green cabbage

50g (2oz) shredded red cabbage

1 celery stick, finely chopped

90g (3oz) finely sliced red pepper

40g (1½oz) finely chopped spring onion

50g (2oz) grated mature Cheddar cheese

1 teaspoon poppy seeds

1 teaspoon sesame seeds

½ teaspoon low-carb vegetable bouillon powder

2 tablespoons Mayonnaise (see page 98)

fresh lemon juice, to taste (optional)

Salade Niçoise with Mustard and Soured-Cream Dressing

Serves 1
Carbs 6.8g
Fat 36g
Protein 34.9g

1. First make the dressing. Blend the oil, mustard, vinegar and soured cream until smooth. Season with salt and pepper then taste and adjust the seasoning as necessary.

2. Arrange the lettuce on a plate. Gently toss the tuna, tomato, anchovies, capers, green beans, red onion, olives and parsley in the dressing then pile them on the lettuce. Garnish with the egg quarters.

40g (1½oz) shredded cos lettuce

185g (7oz) can tuna in water, drained

1 tomato, cut into thin slices

2 anchovy fillets, finely chopped

1 tablespoon capers

40g (1½oz) chopped green beans, steamed until just tender

1 tablespoon chopped red onion

6 black olives

1 tablespoon chopped flat leaf parsley

1 hard-boiled egg, cut into quarters, to garnish

Mustard and soured-cream dressing

1 tablespoon olive oil or flaxseed oil

½ teaspoon coarse grain mustard

1 tablespoon red wine vinegar

1 tablespoon soured cream

salt and pepper

Turkey and Broccoli Salad

Serves 1
Carbs 10g
Fat 19g
Protein 35g

1. Put the turkey breast, broccoli, spring onion, green pepper and tarragon in a bowl. Add the mayonnaise, lemon juice and mustard and combine evenly. Season with salt and pepper and serve.

75–125g (2½–4oz) cooked turkey breast, finely chopped

175g (6oz) raw, finely chopped broccoli

40g (1½oz) finely chopped spring onion

40g (1½oz) finely chopped green pepper

1 teaspoon chopped fresh tarragon or pinch of dried tarragon

1 tablespoon Mayonnaise (see page 98)

2 teaspoons fresh lemon juice

1 teaspoon Dijon mustard

salt and pepper

Pork and Spinach Stir-Fry

1 teaspoon white sesame seeds

125g (4oz) pork loin, cut into thick strips

1 garlic clove, finely sliced

75g (2½oz) finely sliced spring onion

¼ teaspoon cayenne pepper

1 tablespoon olive oil or coconut oil

1 tablespoon Japanese soy sauce/shoshoyu

150g (5oz) roughly chopped raw spinach

1 teaspoon sesame oil

Serves 1
Carbs 6g
Fat 27g
Protein 30g

1. Toast the sesame seeds in a dry pan over a high heat for about 1–2 minutes until golden brown. Remove from the pan and set aside.

2. Combine the pork, garlic, spring onion and cayenne pepper.

3. Heat the olive or coconut oil in a heavy-based pan and stir-fry the pork mixture over a high heat until golden brown and cooked through. Remove from the pan and set aside. Add the soy sauce and spinach to the pan and toss lightly. Cover and cook for about 2 minutes until the spinach is just soft. Return the pork to the pan, add the sesame oil and sesame seeds, toss well and serve.

1 tablespoon coriander seeds

2 teaspoons cumin seeds

1 teaspoon black peppercorns

2 teaspoons shrimp paste (blachan)

8 large chillies, roughly chopped

20 red Asian shallots, small red onions or shallots

5cm (2in) piece of galangal or ginger, chopped

12 small garlic cloves, chopped

75g (2½oz) chopped coriander leaves

6 kaffir lime leaves, shredded

3 lemongrass stems, white part only, finely chopped

2 teaspoons grated lime rind

2 teaspoons salt

2 tablespoons olive oil or coconut oil

Green Curry Paste

Makes 500g (1lb)
Per tablespoon:
Carbs 1.8g
Fat 2g
Protein 1g

1. Toast the coriander and cumin seeds in a dry pan over a medium heat for 2–3 minutes, shaking constantly. Put the roasted seeds and peppercorns in a mortar and pound with a pestle until finely ground.

2. Wrap the shrimp paste in a small piece of foil and cook under a hot grill for 5 minutes, turning twice.

3. Put the ground spices and shrimp paste in a food processor or blender and blend for 5 seconds. Add the chillies, shallots, galangal or ginger, garlic, coriander leaves, lime leaves, lemongrass, lime rind, salt and olive or coconut oil and blend for 10 seconds at a time, scraping down the sides of the bowl with a spatula after each blending, until you have a smooth paste.

Thai Prawn Soup

Serves 4
Carbs 9g
Fat 30g
Protein 40g

5cm (2in) piece of galangal or ginger, cut into very thin slices

500ml (1 pint) coconut milk

250ml (8fl oz) chicken or vegetable stock

2 tablespoons Thai fish sauce

6 kaffir lime leaves

1–2 tablespoons freshly made Green Curry Paste (see opposite) or ready-made curry paste

To serve (per person)

1 tablespoon chopped spring onion

40g (1½oz) sliced raw mushrooms

90g (3oz) finely chopped broccoli

75g (2½oz) raw prawns

1 teaspoon fresh lime juice

2 teaspoons chopped coriander leaves

1. To make the soup base, combine the galangal or ginger, coconut milk, stock, fish sauce, lime leaves and curry paste in a saucepan, bring to the boil and simmer for 10 minutes, stirring occasionally.

2. To make the Thai prawn soup, add the spring onions, mushrooms and broccoli to the hot soup base, then simmer for 5-6 minutes until the vegetables are cooked but still crunchy.

3. Add the prawns and simmer for 3-5 minutes until they are pink and cooked through. Stir in the lime juice and fresh coriander and serve.

TIP

If you want to stockpile for the freezer, allow the soup base to cool at the end of step 1.It can then be stored in a plastic container and frozen.

Lamb Chops with Aubergine Salad

Serves 1
Carbs 6.6g
Fat 30g
Protein 32.5g

1. First make the aubergine salad. Brush the aubergine slices with a little of the oil and cook them on a preheated hot grill, turning them once, until golden and tender. Cut them into quarters.
2. Mix together the remaining oil, vinegar, garlic, lemon juice, cumin and coriander. Season with salt and pepper and mix thoroughly. Add the warm aubergines, stir then cover and chill for 2 hours.
3. Season the lamb with the cumin, salt and pepper. Brush with oil, place under a preheated hot grill and grill for about 5–6 minutes on each side, until cooked through.
4. To serve, add the tomato and cucumber to the aubergine salad and sprinkle with the chopped parsley. Serve the lamb with the aubergine salad and mint raita (see opposite).

TIP
The aubergine salad should be made at least 2 hours in advance and kept in the refrigerator until required.

3 small lamb chops or 2 medium or 125g (4oz) lamb fillet

¼ teaspoon cumin powder

olive or coconut oil for cooking

salt and pepper

Aubergine salad

½ medium aubergine, finely sliced

1 tablespoon olive oil

1 teaspoon red wine vinegar

1 garlic clove, crushed

1 teaspoon fresh lemon juice

generous pinch of ground cumin

generous pinch of ground coriander

1 small tomato, sliced

40g (1½oz) finely chopped cucumber

salt and pepper

1 teaspoon chopped flat leaf parsley, to garnish

Mint Raita

250ml (8fl oz) natural yogurt

20g (¾oz) chopped mint

pinch of cayenne pepper

Serves 4
Carbs 3.9g
Fat 0.6g
Protein 3.2g

1. To make the mint raita, mix together the yogurt and mint with the cayenne pepper. Cover and chill.

Chicken Soup

Serves 8
Carbs 5.5g
Fat 25g
Protein 36g

1 large chicken – about 2.25kg (5lb) – cut into quarters and trimmed of excess fat and skin

3 onions

3 carrots

3 celery sticks

6 garlic cloves

4 bay leaves

1 tablespoon organic chicken or vegetable bouillon powder

4 tablespoons chopped parsley

salt and pepper

1. Place the chicken in a large saucepan with 1 quartered onion, 1 quartered carrot, 1 quartered celery stick, the garlic cloves and bay leaves and cover with water. Bring to the boil then simmer for 1 hour, or until the meat pulls away from the bones.

2. Lift the chicken pieces out of the pan with a slotted spoon and allow to cool. Remove the onion, carrot, celery and garlic and reserve. Pull the chicken off the bones and chop it into bite-sized pieces. Set aside.

3. Skim away any fat from the surface of the stock, then return the chicken bones to the pan. Add about 500ml/1 pint water, bring to the boil, cover and simmer for 1 hour.

4. Strain the stock through a sieve and return the liquid to the pan.

5. Put the reserved cooked vegetables into a food processor or blender with a spoonful of the liquid and blend until smooth, then return to the pan.

6. Finely chop the remaining onions, carrots and celery and add them to the stock. Add the bouillon powder and cook for 20 minutes until the vegetables are tender.

7. Add the chicken pieces and parsley, season with salt and pepper and cook until the chicken is heated through.

8. Divide the soup into eight portions. When cool, these can be stored in plastic containers and frozen, then served whenever you need a low-carb meal in a hurry.

Ginger Poached Cod with Confetti Cabbage

125ml (8fl oz) white wine

1 tablespoon water

25g (1oz) finely chopped spring onions

squeeze of lemon juice

1 teaspoon minced ginger

175g (6oz) cod fillet

Confetti cabbage

1 tablespoon olive oil

100g (3½oz) shredded cabbage

25g (1oz) diced celery

50g (2oz) roasted, peeled and chopped red pepper

1 tablespoon diced white onion

1 tablespoon water

1 tablespoon cider vinegar

¼ teaspoon caraway seeds

salt and pepper

Serves 1
Carbs 8.5g
Fat 1.5g
Protein 32.5g

1. Put the wine, water, spring onions, lemon juice and ginger into a nonstick pan. Bring to the boil then reduce the heat and simmer for 10 minutes.

2. Add the cod and simmer for approximately 8 minutes, until the fish flakes when tested with a fork.

3. To cook the cabbage, heat a wok, then add the oil and heat it. Throw in the cabbage, celery, red pepper, onion, water, vinegar and caraway seeds and season with salt and pepper. Cook, tossing and stirring, for approximately 5 minutes, until all the vegetables are crisp.

4. To serve, arrange the cabbage on a warm plate and place the cod on top.

Salmon Fillet with Anchovy and Rosemary Salsa

Serves 1
Carbs 5g
Fat 33g
Protein 30.4

150g (5oz) salmon fillet

Anchovy and
rosemary salsa

1 tablespoon rosemary

6 anchovy fillets

juice of 1 lemon

**75ml (2½fl oz) olive oil, or a
mix of olive and flaxseed oil**

To serve

**150g (5oz) green beans,
topped and tailed**

1 garlic clove, crushed

salt and pepper

1. First make the salsa. Crush the rosemary in a mortar. Add the anchovies and pound to a paste. Slowly add the lemon juice and then the oil, stirring to blend the salsa.
2. Lightly brush a griddle pan with olive oil. Place the salmon skin side down on the pan and cook over a high heat for about 1–2 minutes, then reduce the heat to medium.
3. Meanwhile, put the beans into a small saucepan with about 2.5cm/1in boiling water, the garlic and a little salt. Cover the pan and cook for 3–4 minutes on a medium heat.
4. When the salmon looks nearly cooked through, flip it over very carefully and cook for a further 1 minute.
5. Remove the lid from the beans and cook on a high heat until the liquid has evaporated.
6. To serve, pile the beans on to a plate, place the salmon on top, skin side up, drizzle with the salsa and serve.

Baked Tuna with Tomato and Herbs

Serves 1
Carbs 8g
Fat 20g
Protein 31g

1. Make little incisions in the tuna steak and insert some garlic, coriander seeds and mint.

2. To make the sauce, heat some of the oil in a saucepan, add the garlic, chilli, oregano and any coriander seeds remaining from the tuna steak and cook, stirring, until the garlic turns golden brown. Add the mint, wine and tomato and cook over a medium heat for 5–10 minutes.

3. Heat the remaining oil in a small flameproof casserole on the hob. Add the tuna and seal on both sides. Pour the sauce over the tuna, season with salt and pepper and transfer to a preheated oven, 220°C/425°F/Gas Mark 7, and cook for 15–20 minutes.

4. Sprinkle the baked tuna with a little mint and the capers. A dish of steamed spinach, spring greens or broccoli would make a good accompaniment.

125g (4oz) fresh tuna steak

½ large garlic clove, cut into fine slivers

1 teaspoon lightly ground coriander seeds

1 tablespoon finely chopped mint, plus more to serve

1 teaspoon capers

salt and pepper

Tomato and herb sauce

1 tablespoon olive oil

½ large garlic clove, finely chopped

¼ teaspoon crumbled dried red chilli (optional)

½ teaspoon dried oregano

1 tablespoon roughly chopped mint

2 tablespoons dry white wine

1 large tomato, skinned, deseeded and roughly chopped

Keep on Tracking

Keep on Tracking principles

This plan will:

◆ Continue to stabilize your blood-sugar levels

◆ Gradually incorporate a higher level of carbohydrates into your diet by moving to a ratio of 35 per cent protein/35 per cent carbohydrate/ 30 per cent fat.

This is also a great plan for someone who doesn't have a lot of weight to lose and therefore doesn't need to start off on the Fast-Track Plan. Lypolisis strips measure ketones in the urine (see page 53). By using lipolysis testing strips, which are available from pharmacies and good health stores, you can keep your carbohydrates to a level that still enables you to lose weight steadily. However, as soon you increase your carbohydrates to more than 50g (2oz) per day, you won't see any real change on the strips and should judge your progress by how your clothes fit and how you feel.

The carbohydrate level that will enable you to lose weight varies from person to person. If you are relatively sedentary or particularly insulin-resistant, you may have to stabilize at around 50–60g (2–2¼oz) of carbohydrates for a while and keep your protein ratio at the 120–30g (4oz) mark. Conversely, if you are exercising at least four or five times a week and don't have that much weight to lose, then you will probably see results at around 90g (3oz) of carbohydrates, balanced by 90g (3oz) of protein and 35–40g (1½oz) of fat.

Keep on Tracking rules

During this period you need to:

◆ Eat 90–125g (3–4oz) of protein per day, depending on how steadily you are losing weight

◆ Eat 50–90g (2–3oz) of carbohydrates per day, at least half of which should be eaten raw

◆ Follow the last nine Fast-Track rules (see page 54)

◆ Keep going – you should Keep on Tracking until you reach your target

◆ Add carbohydrate foods back into your diet one at a time (see above right).

Later, in No Backtracking, you will be given a series of guidelines to enable you to craft your own personalized eating plan, geared to creating the best possible balance between your metabolic responses, your tastes and lifestyle, and your total health profile.

As you move from one level to another, add carbohydrate foods back in the order given below, to minimize the blood-sugar surges that could reactivate cravings:

◆ **More salads and startchy vegetables from the list opposite**

◆ **Fresh cheese (including more matured cheese)**

◆ **Seeds and nuts**

◆ **Berries**

◆ **Wine**

◆ **Pulses**

◆ **Fruit other than berries**

◆ **Starchy vegetables**

◆ **Wholegrains**

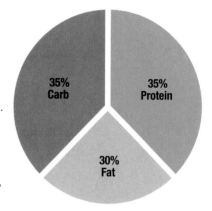

During this phase you should gradually increase your intake of low-density carbohydrates until you reach equal proportions of protein and carbohydrates.

35% Carb

35% Protein

30% Fat

At-a-glance guide

These portions contain roughly 10g (⅓oz) of carbohydrates (all figures are for cooked vegetables, starches and pulses).

Nuts

- 75g (2½oz) almonds
- 40g (1½oz) cashews
- 75g (2½oz) hazelnuts
- 75g (2½oz) macadamias
- 50g (2oz) peanuts, roasted and shelled
- 75g (2½oz) pecans
- 75g (2½oz) pine nuts
- 40g (1½oz) pistachios
- 75g (2½oz) walnuts
- 50g (2oz) pumpkin seeds
- 50g (2oz) sesame seeds
- 50g (2oz) sunflower seeds

Pulses

- 25g (1oz) lentils
- 25g (1oz) kidney beans
- 25g (1oz) black beans
- 25g (1oz) navy beans
- 25g (1oz) lima beans
- 25g (1oz) haricot beans
- 25g (1oz) chickpeas
- 25g (1oz) broad beans
- 25g (1oz) pinto beans

Fruit

- ½ apple
- 12 cherries
- 1 peach
- 12 grapes
- 200g (7oz) strawberries
- ½ grapefruit
- 150g (5oz) cantaloupe melon
- 1 kiwi
- 200g (7oz) watermelon
- 1 plum
- ⅓ banana
- 1 guava
- ⅓ mango

Starchy vegetables

- 75g (2½oz) carrots
- 125g (4oz) winter squash
- 50g (2oz) yam or sweet potato
- 75g (2½oz) peas, shelled
- 50g (2oz) plantain
- 150g (5oz) beetroot
- 50g (2oz) parsnips
- 50g (2oz) white potato

Grains

- 60g (2¼oz) rice, long-grain, brown
- 60g (2¼oz) oatmeal
- 60g (2¼oz) corn kernels
- 1 slice wholewheat bread
- 15g (½oz) wholewheat cereal
- 60g (2¼oz) barley
- 50g (2oz) spinach pasta

The Keep on Tracking Plan

	day & day 1 & 8 2	day & day 9 3 & 10 4	day & day	day & day
BREAKFAST	**Spinach and Cheese Omelette and melon** see page 110, 2 slices of melon **15g carbs** **26g fat** **23g protein**	**Natural yogurt with mixed berries and almonds** 250g (9oz) natural yogurt, 50g (2oz) mixed berries and 25g (1oz) flaked almonds **27g carbs** **21g fat** **7g protein**	**Poached eggs on toast with raw tomato** 2 poached eggs, 1 slice of rye toast and 1 tomato **19g carbs** **12g fat** **15g protein**	**Protein Pancakes** see page 110, serve with 100g (3½oz) strawberries **9.5 g carbs** **17g fat** **15.5g protein**
SNACK	**Sunflower or pumkin seeds** 25g (1oz) sunflower or pumpkin seeds **5g carbs** **14g fat** **6.5g protein**	**Chicken** 100g (3½oz) chicken (hot or cold) **0g carbs** **2g fat** **30g protein**	**Walnuts** 25g (1oz) walnuts **5g carbs** **15g fat** **4g protein**	**Boiled or poached egg** 1 egg **1g carbs** **5.5g fat** **6g protein**
LUNCH	**Moroccan Chicken Salad** see page 86 **4.2g carbs** **28g fat** **31g protein**	**Thai Beef Salad with Chilli Dressing** see page 76 **6g carbs** **18g fat** **24g protein**	**Chicken Soup** see page 67 **5.6g carbs** **25g fat** **36g protein**	**Hake with Roasted Peppers and Anchovy Vinaigrette** see page 78 **7g carbs** **26g fat** **34g protein**
SNACK	**Almonds and olives** 25g (1oz) almonds and 25g (1oz) olives **8g carbs** **20g fat** **5g protein**	**Sunflower or pumpkin seeds** 25g (1oz) sunflower or pumpkin seeds **5g carbs** **14g fat** **6.5g protein**	**Whey Smoothie** see page 60, use 1 scoop of whey-protein powder **3g carbs** **1g fat** **20g protein**	**Hazelnuts** 25g (1oz) hazelnuts **4g carbs** **17g fat** **4g protein**
DINNER	**Marinated Monkfish Kebabs with Mint Raita and Spicy Cauliflower** see pages 79, 67 and 76 **13g carbs** **38g fat** **40g protein**	**Scallops with Mushrooms** see page 80, serve with 125g (4oz) asparagus, green beans and garlic **9g carbs** **16g fat** **25g protein**	**Spicy Fish with Chinese Greens** see page 83 **10g carbs** **33g fat** **31g protein**	**Creamy Prawn Curry** see page 84, serve with 75g (2½oz) raw spinach, 100g (3½oz) chopped tomato and 25g (1oz) onion **20g carbs** **2.2g fat** **29g protein**

BREAKFAST

Whey Smoothie and an apple
see page 60, use 2 scoops of whey-
protein powder
26g carbs
1.5g fat
40g protein

Porridge with apricots and walnuts
125g (4oz) oats with 500ml (1 pint) soya milk or mineral water; 1 fresh apricot and 25g (1oz) walnuts
38g carbs
26g fat
18g protein

Ham with poached eggs and a pear
1 slice organic ham, 2 poached eggs
27g carbs
16g fat
16g protein

SNACK

Cheddar cheese
25g (1oz) Cheddar cheese
0g carbs
9g fat
7g protein

Sunflower or pumpkin seeds
25g (1oz) sunflower or pumpkin seeds
5g carbs
14g fat
6.5g protein

Macadamia nuts
25g (1oz) macadamia nuts
4g carbs
21g fat
2.2g protein

LUNCH

Baked Sardines
see page 84
7g carbs
44g fat
30g protein

Greek Lamb-Burgers
see page 77, serve with 150g (5oz) endive salad
6.3g carbs
41g fat
39g protein

Peppered Venison Steak with Red Cabbage and Onions
see page 85
11g carbs
24g fat
39g protein

SNACK

Pistachio nuts
25g (1oz) pistachios
7g carbs
13g fat
6g protein

Chicken
1 chicken leg (hot or cold)
0g carbs
4g fat
15g protein

Cottage cheese
50g (2oz) cottage cheese
1g carbs
2g fat
7.7g protein

DINNER

Potato skins and guacamole with green salad with bacon
1 potato skin filled with Gaucamole (see page 118), 3 slices crispy bacon, 150g (5oz) green salad
19g carbs
33g fat
8g protein

Bouillabaisse
see page 81
9.6g carbs
23g fat
48g protein

Deli plate:
50g (2oz) mixed cheeses, 125g (4oz) lean meats and 100g (3½oz) celery, chicory and cherry tomatoes
13g carbs
22g fat
52g protein

Thai Beef Salad with Chilli Dressing

Serves 1
Carbs 6g
Fat 18g
Protein 24g

1 garlic clove, finely chopped

1 coriander root, finely chopped

1 tablespoon olive oil

100g (3½oz) rump or sirloin steak

150g (5oz) soft lettuce, washed and roughly torn into pieces

100g (3½oz) halved cherry tomatoes

75g (2½oz) sliced cucumber

40g (1½oz) finely chopped spring onion

1 tablespoon coriander leaves

generous pinch of ground black pepper

Chilli dressing

1 tablespoon Thai fish sauce

1 tablespoon lime juice

1 tablespoon soy sauce or Bragg liquid aminos (available from health-food stores, see page 92)

1 teaspoon finely chopped red chilli

1. Combine the garlic, coriander root, black pepper and half of the oil in a mortar and grind with a pestle until fine. Alternatively use a food processor or blender. Spread the mixture over the steak.
2. Heat the remaining oil in a heavy-based frying pan or wok over a high heat. Add the steak and cook for about 4 minutes on each side, turning it once. Remove from the heat and allow to cool.
3. Arrange the lettuce, tomatoes, cucumber and spring onions on a plate.
4. To make the dressing, mix the fish sauce, lime juice, soy sauce and chilli.
5. Cut the cooled steak into thin strips and arrange on top of the salad. Drizzle over the dressing, scatter with the coriander leaves and serve immediately.

Spicy Cauliflower

325g (12oz) cooked and finely chopped cauliflower

90g (3oz) finely chopped red pepper

1 tablespoon pine nuts

75g (2½oz) finely chopped spring onion

100g (3½oz) finely cubed tomato

1 tablespoon finely chopped mint

Piquant dressing

1 tablespoon olive oil or flaxseed oil

½ teaspoon turmeric

1 tablespoon lemon juice

pinch of cumin

salt and pepper

Serves 1
Carbs 9.5g
Fat 24g
Protein 6g

1. To make the dressing, combine the oil, turmeric, lemon juice and cumin, season with salt and pepper and mix well.
2. Put the cauliflower, red pepper, pine nuts, spring onion, tomato and mint in a bowl. Add the dressing and toss until evenly combined.

Greek Lamb-burger

Serves 6
Per burger:
Carbs 6.3g
Fat 41g
Protein 35g

1 In a bowl, gently combine the lamb, feta and olives. Form the mixture into 6 patties about 2.5cm (1in) thick and season to taste with salt and pepper. Cover and chill for 10 minutes in the refrigerator.

2 Barbecue the lamb-burgers or cook them under a preheated hot grill for about 7 minutes on each side for medium-rare.

3 Serve the lamb-burgers with a green salad and either Baba Ghanoush (see page 114), Creamy Cucumber Salsa (see page 105) or Roasted Tomato and Mint Salsa (see pages 121). Any leftover burgers may be frozen in a plastic container.

1 kg (2lb) minced lamb

50g (2oz) crumbled feta cheese

100g (3½oz) chopped pitted olives

salt and pepper

Hake with Roasted Peppers and Anchovy Vinaigrette

Serves 1
Carbs 7g
Fat 26g
Protein 34g

1 small red pepper

1 small yellow pepper

½ tablespoon olive oil

175g (6oz) hake fillet

1 tablespoon white wine

**1 tablespoon purple
basil leaves**

black pepper

1 lemon wedge, to garnish

Anchovy vinaigrette

**2 anchovy fillets, roughly
chopped**

**½ garlic clove, finely
chopped**

juice of ½ lemon

**1 tablespoon olive oil or
flaxseed oil**

1. Cover a baking sheet with foil. Place the peppers on the baking sheet and bake in a preheated oven, 190°C/375°F/Gas Mark 5, for 40 minutes, turning them once during cooking.

2. Take the peppers out of the oven, put them in a bowl and cover them with clingfilm; this will make the skins easier to remove. When the peppers are cool enough to handle, peel them, discard the seeds and set the flesh aside.

3. To make the vinaigrette, put the anchovies, garlic and lemon juice in a food processor or blender and blend briefly, then add the oil until the dressing looks velvety and smooth.

4. Pour the vinaigrette over the peppers, cover with clingfilm and chill until required. (Up to this stage of the recipe can be prepared a day ahead.)

5. Heat the oil gently in a frying pan, add the hake fillet, skin side down, and sauté for 2 minutes, without allowing the fish to brown. Add the wine to the pan with some of the chopped basil and pepper, tilting the pan to coat the fish. Cook for a further 3–4 minutes, basting the fish occasionally with the juices.

6. Put the marinated peppers on a serving plate and place the fish on top. Drizzle any excess dressing over the fish and scatter with more basil. Serve with a wedge of lemon.

Marinated Monkfish Kebabs

½ onion, grated

1 bay leaf

1 large rosemary sprig

1 garlic clove, crushed

grated rind and juice
of ½ lemon

1 tablespoon olive oil

150g (5oz) monkfish, cut
into cubes

salt and pepper

lemon wedges, to garnish

Serves 1
Carbs 3.5g
Fat 14g
Protein 28g

1. Mix together the onion, herbs, garlic, lemon rind and juice and olive oil. Season with salt and pepper and pour over the monkfish. Cover and leave to marinate for 1 hour.

2. Remove the monkfish from the marinade and thread on to skewers. Place the fish under a preheated hot grill and cook for about 10 minutes, turning occasionally until browned and cooked right through.

3. Serve the monkfish with lemon wedges, Mint Raita (see page 67) and Spicy Cauliflower (see page 76).

Scallops with Mushrooms

4 large scallops, shelled, rinsed and drained

1½ tablespoons olive oil

40g (1½oz) sliced raw chestnut or mixed mushrooms

90g (3oz) chopped red pepper

1 garlic clove, crushed

1 tablespoon chopped parsley

1 teaspoon finely chopped chervil

salt and pepper

Serves 1
Carbs 8g
Fat 16g
Protein 25g

1. Separate any corals from the scallops and set aside. Slice each scallop horizontally into 2 flat discs, then brush them with some of the olive oil. Lightly oil a griddle pan.

2. Heat the remaining oil in a small saucepan then add the mushrooms and red peppers and cook for 5–6 minutes over a medium heat. Season with salt and pepper, then add the scallop corals, garlic, parsley and chervil and cook for a further 2–3 minutes.

3. Meanwhile, heat the griddle pan and, when it is almost smoking, add the scallops and cook them for 1 minute on each side.

4. To serve, toss the scallops into the mushroom mixture and serve at once.

Bouillabaisse

Serves 2
Carbs 9.6g
Fat 23g
Protein 48g

750g (1½lb) mixed fish and shellfish (such as red mullet, monkfish, prawns, clams and whiting)

500ml (1 pint) water or fish stock

pinch of saffron threads

3 tablespoons olive oil

75g (2½oz) finely chopped leek

75g (2½oz) chopped onion

1 celery stick, finely chopped

1 garlic clove, crushed

1 bouquet garni

½ teaspoon orange rind

¼ teaspoon fennel seeds

125g (4oz) skinned and roughly chopped tomatoes

2 teaspoons tomato purée

1 teaspoon Pernod

salt and pepper

1–2 tablespoons chopped parsley, to garnish

1. If using whole fish, remove the heads, tails and fins, then put them into the measured water and boil for 15 minutes to make a fish stock. Strain and reserve the liquid. (Alternatively, you can use a ready-made fish stock, but check the carbohydrate content of the stock.)
2. Cut the fish into large chunks, but leave the shellfish in their shells. Soak the saffron in 1–2 tablespoons hot water.
3. Heat the oil in a large saucepan, add the leeks, onion and celery and cook for 5 minutes until softened.
4. Add the garlic, bouquet garni, orange rind, fennel seeds and tomatoes. Stir in the saffron and its liquid and the fish stock. Bring to the boil then simmer, covered, for 30–40 minutes.
5. Add the fish and shellfish and cook for 6–10 minutes, or until all the fish flake easily and the shellfish have opened. Transfer the fish to a plate with a slotted spoon.
6. Keep the liquid boiling to allow the oil and broth to emulsify, and add the tomato purée and Pernod.
7. Check the seasoning, then pour the soup into bowls. Add the fish to the bowls or serve it separately. Sprinkle the soup with the parsley.

Spicy Fish

Serves 1
Carbs 3.8g
Fat 16g
Protein 26g

1 garlic clove

1 red shallot

1 lemongrass stem, white part only

½ teaspoon ground turmeric

¼ teaspoon ground ginger

½ small red chilli

1 tablespoon coconut oil

1 teaspoon Thai fish sauce

125g (4oz) boneless white fish fillets, cut into bite-sized pieces

salt and pepper

1 tablespoon chopped coriander, to garnish

1. Put the garlic, shallot, lemongrass, turmeric, ginger, chilli and salt and pepper into a food processor or blender and process until a paste is formed, adding the coconut oil and fish sauce to help the grinding.
2. Place the fish in a bowl and toss with the spice paste. Cover and refrigerate for 15 minutes.
3. Thread the pieces of fish on skewers and arrange on a foil-lined tray. Cook under a preheated hot grill for 3–4 minutes, turning it once so that the pieces brown evenly. Serve sprinkled with the coriander.

Chinese Greens

Serves 1
Carbs 6.3g
Fat 17g
Protein 5g

300g (12oz) raw shredded Chinese greens

1 teaspoon peanut oil

½ teaspoon finely chopped garlic

1 teaspoon oyster sauce

1 tablespoon water

½ teaspoon sesame oil

1. Put the greens in a saucepan of boiling water and cook for 1–2 minutes, or until just tender. Drain well, then place on a serving plate.
2. Heat the peanut oil in a small pan and cook the garlic briefly. Stir in the oyster sauce, the measured water and sesame oil, then bring the mixture to the boil and pour it over the greens. Toss together and serve immediately.

TIP

Use a mixture of bok choy, choy sum and Chinese broccoli – or you can substitute spring greens, rocket, spinach and finely chopped broccoli.

Baked Sardines

Serves 1
Carbs 7g
Fat 44g
Protein 30g

1 tablespoon olive oil

4 large fresh sardines, filleted (ask your fishmonger to do this)

½ slice of rye bread, processed into breadcrumbs

grated rind of ½ lemon

25g (1oz) pine nuts

1 small dried chilli, crumbled

1 tablespoon chopped parsley

salt and pepper

lemon wedges, to garnish

1. Brush a baking tray with some of the olive oil and place 4 sardine fillets (2 sardines), skin side down, very close to each other. Sprinkle the sardines with half of the rye crumbs, lemon rind, pine nuts, dried chilli, parsley and salt and pepper. Place the other 4 sardine fillets directly on top, skin side up. Sprinkle with the rest of the rye crumbs, lemon rind, pine nuts, dried chilli, parsley, salt and pepper.
2. Drizzle the sardines with the remaining olive oil and bake in a preheated oven, 200°C/400°F/Gas Mark 6, for 6–8 minutes.
3. Serve with lemon wedges and a tomato and onion salad.

Creamy Prawn Curry

2 teaspoons coconut oil

75g (2½oz) finely chopped onion

1 garlic clove, crushed

½ teaspoon turmeric

½ small red chilli, deseeded and finely chopped

4 curry leaves or 1 teaspoon medium curry powder

125ml (4fl oz) coconut milk

150g (5oz) raw king prawns, shelled and deveined

salt

1 tablespoon chopped coriander or curry leaves, to garnish

Serves 1
Carbs 14g
Fat 2.5g
Protein 29g

1. Heat the coconut oil in a pan, add the onion and cook until soft. Add the garlic, turmeric, chilli and curry leaves or curry powder and stir over a medium heat for 1 minute. Pour in the coconut milk, season with salt and simmer for 10 minutes.
2. Add the prawns and cook for 8 minutes, or until the prawns are tender.
3. Garnish the prawns with curry leaves or chopped coriander leaves.

Peppered Venison Steak with Red Cabbage and Onions

175g (6oz) venison steak

½ tablespoon olive oil

150g (5oz) finely chopped red onion

200g (7oz) finely sliced red cabbage

125ml (4 fl oz) red wine

100g (3½oz) sliced eating apple

1 tablespoon coconut oil

salt and cracked black pepper

Serves 1
Carbs 11g
Fat 24g
Protein 39g

1. Place the venison between two sheets of clingfilm and pound with a chef's mallet or rolling pin until it is 1cm (½in) thick and tenderized. Sprinkle each side liberally with cracked black pepper and set aside.

2. Heat the olive oil in a heavy-based saucepan and gently fry the onion and cabbage for 30 minutes until softened.

3. Add the red wine and apple slices, then cover the pan and simmer for 30 minutes. Season with salt and pepper to taste.

4. Heat the coconut oil in a separate pan and cook the venison on a medium to high heat for about 3–4 minutes on each side for medium, or slightly longer if you like your meat well done.

5. Make a bed of red cabbage and serve the venison on top.

Moroccan Chicken Salad

Serves 2
Carbs 4.2g
Fat 28g
Protein 31g

2 chicken breasts, skinned and boned

150g (5oz) chilled, shredded cos lettuce

150g (5oz) chilled, shredded radicchio lettuce

1–2 tablespoons Lemon Cumin Dressing (see opposite)

½ large avocado, peeled and thinly sliced

1 tablespoon chopped coriander leaves

Orange and coriander marinade

2 tablespoons olive oil

½ tablespoon lemon juice

½ tablespoon orange juice

2 garlic cloves, chopped

½ teaspoon ground coriander

½ teaspoon ground cumin

¼ teaspoon cinnamon

¼ teaspoon chopped oregano leaves

¼ teaspoon salt

1. Place the chicken breasts in a glass dish.

2. Make the marinade, mixing all the ingredients together in a small bowl. Reserve 2 tablespoons for basting and pour the rest over the chicken, turning it so that it is coated thoroughly, then cover and refrigerate for 20 minutes.

3. Remove the chicken from the marinade and place it on a foil-covered baking tray. Put the tray on a rack and place it about 15 cm (6in) below a preheated grill. Cook the chicken, turning it and brushing it with the reserved marinade, for about 10 minutes or until a fork will easily go into the chicken and the juices run clear.

4. Put the shredded cos and red-leaf lettuces in a large bowl. Toss with 1–2 tablespooms of the dressing then arrange on a large platter. Cut the chicken breasts into 1cm (½in) slices and set them on the lettuce. Garnish with the avocado slices. Pour the remaining dressing over the chicken and sprinkle with the chopped coriander leaves.

Lemon Cumin Dressing

2 tablespoons lemon juice

½ teaspoon soy sauce

1 teaspoon ground cumin

6 tablespoons olive oil

Makes 75ml (2½fl oz)
Carbs 0.8g
Fat 0.2g
Protein trace

1. Combine all the ingredients in a bowl and mix together thoroughly.

No Backtracking

No Backtracking principles

This is a plan for life. You will carefully reintroduce certain carbohydrates into your diet – and find the balance that maintains your weight and keeps you feeling trim. This crucial phase will allow you to:

◆ Establish the carbohydrate levels that you can eat in order to remain slim and supply your energy requirements

◆ Break totally with bad habits made in the past

◆ Never return to yo-yo dieting

◆ Find a healthy attitude to food and a viable eating plan for the rest of your life.

No Backtracking rules

During this phase you need to:

◆ Increase your daily carb intake by no more than 10g (⅓oz) each week

◆ Add new foods one at a time

◆ Eliminate a new food if it provokes weight gain; a return of physical symptoms lost during the Fast-Track Plan; increased appetite, cravings or water retention

◆ Drop back to the next-lowest level of carbohydrate intake if you gain weight

◆ Carry on eating adequate amounts of healthy fats and lean protein at every meal to ensure a balanced diet

◆ Continue to take vitamin and mineral supplements regularly, drink masses of water and, of course, exercise regularly.

Make this diet the one that works

Once you have reached your target weight, you can start on the No Backtracking plan. Increase your intake of carbohydrates by 5–10 grams per day until you reach your optimum level for weight management (see pages 90–91). This will probably be around 40 per cent of your total daily calorific intake, but remember that everybody differs, especially when you consider activity levels.

If you have high insulin resistance, then you may have to Keep on Tracking and be careful about how many carbohydrates you consume on a daily basis. But if you're one of the lucky ones with low insulin resistance, you may be able to eat most vegetables (including starchy vegetables), fruit, pulses and wholegrains such as oats, barley, millet, wild rice, couscous and buckwheat. You can also begin to use recipes containing carbohydrate ingredients such as

THINK POSITIVE!

Well done, you've reached your target weight. Think about how much better you feel now that you have lost the weight and remember this feeling whenever you are tempted to slip back into your old eating habits.

breadcrumbs; you may even be able to handle an occasional potato. But don't eat all these things in one day. You still have to monitor your carbohydrate intake to stay where you are – healthy and energized. Remember the eating habits that got you here in the first place. You should have successfully gauged your ideal carbohydrate level, and be maintaining a stable weight and energy levels, within 4–12 weeks of following the No Backtracking plan.

Stick to the basic weight management tips (see pages 44–45) and try to be good 80 per cent of the time. We are all allowed the odd slip up – if you want a slab of chocolate cake from time to time, make sure it is the best you find and enjoy it. If you ever see the scales creeping up, cut back, even go back to the Fast Track plan for a few days until your weight is back to normal, and then gradually raise your carbohydrate levels once again.

A template for life

Two portions of higher GI carbohydrates are included per day on the suggested eating plan (see page 94). Treat this as the template you ought to follow from now on. And try some of these tricks to keep your carbohydrates at a moderate, healthy level:

◆ Opt for rye bread, oatcakes and rye crackers instead of wheat-based bread. Even if you are not wheat-intolerant, it is worth considering this.

◆ Eat fruit 20 minutes before eating anything else, not afterwards. Fruit takes less time to digest, but if eaten on top of a heavy meal, can cause bloating.

◆ If you are going to drink alcohol, choose dry white wine or, even better, red, which contains flavonoids with antioxidant and anti-platelet properties thought to reduce deaths from coronary artery disease. If you have managed to kick the alcohol habit, opt for grape juice, which contains flavonoids similar to those in red wine.

◆ Mix sweet potato with cauliflower as a mash or purée to go with roast chicken. The aim is to mix a high GI vegetable with a low one, to reduce the total carbohydrate level.

◆ When making a rice dish such as risotto, reverse your ratio of vegetables to rice: add a little rice to a heap of vegetables. And try grating raw vegetables such as carrots and courgettes into the dish at the last moment – it adds texture and you get the benefit of all those raw phytonutrients.

◆ Don't give up on those whey-protein smoothies – they are still the most effective way of getting high-value biological protein.

Make carb cravings a thing of the past – never let refined carbohydrates into your cupboards again.

Basic weight-management

If you are trying to maintain and stabilize your weight at a certain level, then you need to be able to calculate exactly how much fat, protein and carbohydrate you should be eating each day. The following boxes give you all the information you need to work out your daily requirements for fat, protein and carboydrates.

Daily calorific intake

To work out your ideal daily calorific intake, multiply your weight in pounds x 10 if you are quite sedentary or 15 if you are more active.

For example, if you weigh 154lb (70kg) and don't exercise, you should stabilize at around 1,540 kilocalories per day; if you are quite active, then you will need to take in around 2,310 kilocalories. Athletes and very active people will usually need to take in even more calories in order to remain balanced.

Daily protein requirements

Protein provides 4 kilocalories per gram and your daily protein requirement depends upon your current level of body fat. To calculate how many grams of protein you should eat each day follow the equation below and refer to the table below that for your physical activity factor:

Weight in kilograms x % body fat = total body-fat weight (Weight in pounds divided by 2.2 x % body fat = total body fat weight)

Weight in kilograms - total body-fat weight = lean body mass (Weight in pounds divided by 2.2 – total body fat = lean body mass)

Lean body mass x 2.2 x physical activity factor = grams of protein per day

Total daily protein requirement in grams x 4 = daily kilocalories that should come from protein

Physical activity factor	
Sedentary	0.5
Light (walks occasionally)	0.6
Moderate (30 minutes 3 times per week)	0.7
Active (1 hour 5 times per week)	0.8
Very active (2 hours 5 times per week)	0.9
Body-building (heavy training twice a day, 5 times per week)	1

Daily fat requirements

To work out your fat requirements, you need to know that fat provides 9 kilocalories per gram and that 30 per cent of your daily calorific intake should come from fat. To work out how many grams of fat you should eat each day you need to make the following calculations:

> **Daily calorific intake x 30 per cent = daily kilocalories that should come from fat**
>
> **Daily kilocalories that should come from fat ÷ 9 = total daily fat requirement in grams**

Daily carbohydrate requirements

Carbohydrates provide 4 kilocalories per gram. To work out how many grams of carbohydrate you should eat each day you need to make the following calculations:

> **Daily calorific intake - daily kilocalories that should come from fat and protein = daily kilocalories that should come from carbohydrate**
>
> **Daily kilocalories that should come from carbohydrate ÷ 4 = grams of carbohydrate per day**

Adjusting your diet ratio to suit you

This ratio of protein to carbohydrates may not, of course, be perfect for you. If you feel happier on a more equal ratio of protein to carbohydrates, then add the amounts of protein and carbohydrates together and divide them by two. You will have to experiment until you find a level with which you feel comfortable, and which keeps you feeling slim and energized.

daily calorific intake

daily protein requirement

daily fat requirement

daily carb requirement

Guidelines for life

Keys to long-term dietary success

- Kiss goodbye to refined and high GI carbs.
- Go for natural and organic foods whenever possible.
- Aim for maximum fibre, by eating as many as possible of your fruit and vegetables raw.
- Don't touch soft drinks, alcohol and fruit juices, especially on the Fast-Track Plan; reintroduce alcohol in moderation on the Keep on Tracking Plan.
- Rev up your intake of omega-3 fatty acids from fish and flaxseed oil (see page 32).
- Banish vegetable oils and hydrogenated fats – switch instead to cold-pressed olive oil.
- Include protein at all meals, and snacks that are rich in omega-6 fatty acids (see page 32).
- Take absolutely no trans fats – so no deep-fried food, margarines and processed junk food.
- Remember to take your supplements for optimum health (see pages 46–47).
- Keep on exercising (both aerobic and resistance training) at least four days per week.

RESTAURANT BASICS

No breadcrumbs, and be careful with sauces. Don't be afraid to ask questions: restaurants are used to this.

- **Don't have commercial dressings – use oil and lemon juice instead.**
- **Say no to bread rolls and croutons.**
- **Ask for your main course to be grilled, steamed, sautéed or poached, with a couple of portions of vegetables and salad. When you are on the Fast Track, don't choose potatoes, corn, peas, carrots and beetroot, as these are high GI foods.**
- **If you have moved on to Keep on Tracking, eat these in extreme moderation and count as two servings. Instead, go for lower GI choices, such as broccoli, cauliflower, green beans and asparagus.**

Shopping list

To avoid running out to the shops every five minutes, or substituting some ingredient that you shouldn't, do a bit of shopping in advance and ensure that you have the following:

Supermarket	Tofu	Fresh coriander, basil, mint,	Flaxseed oil (an excellent source
Coconut milk	Soya milk	rosemary	of omega-3 fatty acids; needs to
Coconut oil (very stable for cooking	Small cans of water-packed	**Health-food store**	be kept refrigerated)
and a good substitute for other	tuna/sardines/oysters/mussels	Micro-filtered whey-protein	Psyllium husks
oils)	Small pots of cottage cheese	powder (see page 28)	**Pharmacist**
Fresh ginger	Sesame seeds	Supplements (see page 47)	Lypolisis strips are available
Limes/lemons	Coriander seeds	Liquid aminos (like soy sauce, but	from chemists and most good
Fresh garlic	Cumin	with no added salt, wheat or	health stores. They are useful
Sunflower seeds	Fennel seeds	gluten; a great source of amino	for measuring ketones in the
Pumpkin seeds	Eggs	acids; made by Bragg)	urine.

Eating out

You don't have to be a hermit just because you are on a diet, but try not to go somewhere that is 'carboholic' heaven, such as a pizza-and-pasta restaurant or fast-food outlet. Most restaurants are fine – it's just a case of knowing what to pick and keeping temptation at bay.

Good restaurant choices

Italian Restaurant	**Starters:** Antipasto plate, grilled calamari, prawns in garlic, prosciutto with Parmesan, carpaccio **Main courses:** Grilled chicken, fish, steak, veal cutlets, chicken piccata **Vegetables:** Salad, courgettes, aubergines, peppers
Indian Restaurant	**Starters:** Chicken tikka, tandoori chicken or prawns **Main courses:** Most curries with meat or fish, but no potato or rice; spinach with paneer **Vegetables:** Cucumber raita, salad
Chinese Restaurant	Ask for no sugar and monosodium glutamate in sauces. **Starters:** Chicken or prawn satay **Main courses:** Steamed fish, Peking duck without pancakes **Vegetables:** Stir-fries with snow peas, ginger, bean sprouts, bok choy
Japanese Restaurant	**Starters:** Sashimi (raw fish), miso soup **Main courses:** Meat or fish teppenyaki, tofu **Vegetables:** Grilled vegetables – no sauce
Spanish Restaurant	**Starters:** Gazpacho, mushrooms in garlic, fresh anchovies, prawns, scallops wrapped in bacon **Main courses:** Grilled fish, squid, meat **Vegetables:** Salads, green beans with garlic
Thai Restaurant	Ask for no sugar in sauces. **Starters:** Tom Ka Khai (chicken soup with coconut, or ask for it to be made with prawns) **Main courses:** Most curries made with coconut and fresh Thai curry pastes **Vegetables:** Amazing salads with a spicy kick – watch out for added noodles
French Restaurant	**Starters:** Asparagus with hollandaise sauce, steamed mussels, oysters **Main courses:** Poached salmon, bouillabaisse, chicken, grilled steak or lamb **Vegetables:** Mixed vegetables or *salade verte*
Greek Restaurant	**Starters:** Olives, tzatziki with crudités **Main courses:** Souvla, kleftiko, chicken kebabs **Vegetables:** Greek salad with feta

The No Backtracking Plan

	day & day 1 & 2	day & day 2 & 3	day & day 3 & 4	day & day 4 & 1
BREAKFAST	**Poached eggs on toast with raw tomato** 2 poached eggs, 1 slice of rye toast and 1 tomato **19g carbs** **12g fat** **15g protein**	**Fruit salad with yogurt** 150g (5oz) fruit salad and 250g (9oz) yogurt **27g carbs** **4g fat** **6g protein**	**Whey Smoothie with Berries** see page 60, use 2 scoops of whey-protein powder with 60g (2¼oz) raspberries **20g carbs** **1g fat** **40g protein**	**Bacon and mushrooms with raw tomato and watercress** 50g (2oz) bacon,150g (5oz) mushrooms, raw tomato and watercress **8g carbs** **8g fat** **11g protein**
SNACK	**Sunflower or pumpkin seeds** 25g (1oz) sunflower or pumpkin seeds **5g carbs** **14g fat** **6.5g protein**	**Walnuts** 25g (1oz) walnuts **5g carbs** **17g fat** **4g protein**	**Boiled egg** 1 egg **1g carbs** **5.5g fat** **6g protein**	**Almonds** 25g (1oz) almonds **5g carbs** **15g fat** **6g protein** **20g protein**
LUNCH	**Spicy Roasted Aubergine and Creamy Cucumber Salsa** see pages 101 and 105, serve with 50g (2oz) cooked brown rice **28.6 carbs** **17g fat** **10g protein**	**Chicken Ratatouille** see page 99, serve with ½ jacket potato **43g carbs** **31g fat** **42g protein**	**Hummus with pinenuts, crudités and rye toast** see page 117, 15g (½oz) pine nuts, crudités and 1 slice rye toast **30g carbs** **35g fat** **16g protein**	**Energy-Booster Soup** see page 112, serve with 2 rye crackers and 15g (½oz) peanut butter **30g carbs** **13g fat** **50g protein**
SNACK	**Apple and cheese** 1 apple and 25g (1oz) Cheddar cheese **21g carbs** **9.5g fat** **7g protein**	**Whey Smoothie** see page 60, use 1 scoop of whey-protein powder **3g carbs** **1g fat** **20g protein**	**Pear and macadamia nuts** 1 pear and 25g (1oz) macadamias **29g carbs** **21g fat** **3g protein**	**Fish Pâté with celery** see page 97, ½ portion of Fish Pâté on a celery stick **4g carbs** **8g fat** **15g protein**
DINNER	**Moroccan Lamb with Orange and Chickpeas** see page 102, serve with watercress and rocket salad **18g carbs** **19g fat** **31g protein**	**Omelette Arnold Bennett with a green salad** see page 96 **5g carbs** **37g fat** **37g protein**	**Salmon steak with Chicory and Radicchio Gratin** See page 97, 125g (4oz) salmon steak **5.7g carbs** **25g fat** **40g protein**	**Chicken and Roquefort Caesar Salad** see page 98 **4g carbs** **45g fat** **37g protein**

Porridge with apricots and walnuts 25g (1oz) oatmeal with 300ml (½ pint) soya milk or mineral water; and 15g (½oz) apricots and walnuts **27g carbs** **18g fat** **14g protein**	**Ham and pineapple with raw tomato** 150g (5oz) fresh pineapple, 75g (2½oz) ham and 1 tomato **24g carbs** **18g fat** **12g protein**	**Smoked salmon and poached egg with rye toast** 2–3 slices smoked salmon, 1 poached egg and 1 slice rye toast **13g carbs** **19g carbs** **42g protein**	**BREAKFAST**
Chicken 100g (3½oz) chicken, hot or cold **0g carbs** **2g fat** **30g protein**	**Whey Smoothie** see page 60, use 1 scoop of whey- protein powder **3g carbs** **1g fat** **20g protein**	**Peach** 1 peach **10g carbs** **0g fat** **0.5g protein**	**SNACK**
Baked Courgettes with Goats' Cheese and Mint see page 104, serve with lamb's lettuce and broad beans **15g carbs** **37g fat** **10g protein**	**Crunchy Rice Salad** see page 100 **30g carbs** **14g fat** **11g protein**	**Sweet Potato and Cauliflower Purée** see page 101, serve with 125g (4oz) roast chicken breast and broccoli **25g carbs** **6g fat** **42g protein**	**LUNCH**
Walnuts 25g (1oz) walnuts **5g carbs** **15g fat** **4g protein**	**Whey Smoothie** see page 60, use 1 scoop of whey- protein powder **3g carbs** **1g fat** **20g protein**	**Olives** 50g (2oz) olives **0g carbs** **6g fat** **0.5g protein**	**SNACK**
Steak, new potatoes and vegetables with garlic mayonnaise 125g (4oz) lean steak, garlic mayonnaise (see page 98), 2 small new potatoes and green vegetables **30g carbs** **23g fat** **39g protein**	**Steamed Mussels with Lemongrass, Basil and Wine** see page 105, serve with 225g (7½oz) large mixed salad **10g carbs** **5.3g fat** **12g protein**	**Deli plate** 50g (2oz) Camembert, crudités, 2 oatcakes and 50g (2oz) grapes **33g carbs** **25g fat** **22g protein**	**DINNER**

Omelette Arnold Bennett

Serves 1
Carbs 1.2g
Fat 37g
Protein 37g

75g (2½oz) smoked haddock

300ml (½ pint) fish stock

1 tablespoon grated
Parmesan cheese

3 eggs

1 tablespoon cold water

15g (½oz) butter

1 tablespoon double cream

salt and black pepper

1. Gently poach the haddock in the fish stock for 7–8 minutes or until just tender. Allow to cool then remove any skin and bones.

2. Mix the flaked haddock with the cheese and season with salt and pepper. Put the eggs into a bowl and lightly beat with the water.

3. Melt the butter in an omelette pan and pour in the egg mixture. When the eggs begin to set, put the fish and cheese on top of them. While they are still liquid, pour over the cream then put the pan under a preheated hot grill for a few minutes until the top is golden brown. Do not fold the omelette but slide it on to a hot plate and serve immediately.

Fish Pâté with Baby Gems

Serves 1
Carbs 6.7g
Fat 16.5g
Protein 30

3 baby gem lettuces, split into halves

Fish pâté

125g (4oz) can oily fish, such as salmon, mackerel, sardines or tuna

1 small red onion, finely chopped

1 garlic clove, finely chopped

1 tablespoon white wine vinegar

1 tablespoon finely chopped parsley

1 teaspoon lemon juice

black pepper

¼ cucumber, finely sliced, to garnish

1. Put the canned fish, red onion, garlic, vinegar and parsley in a food processor or blender and blend until well combined, but still with a bit of texture. Add the lemon juice and pepper to taste, then cover and chill for 20 minutes

2. Serve the pâté spread over the cut side of the baby gem lettuces. Top with the cucumber slices.

Chicory and Radicchio Gratin

1 head radicchio, quartered lengthways

1 head chicory, quartered lengthways

1 teaspoon pesto sauce

1 tablespoon olive oil

25g (1oz) grated Emmental cheese

pinch of nutmeg

salt and pepper

Serves 1
Carbs 5.5g
Fat 25g
Protein 10g

1. Grease a small baking dish and arrange the radicchio and chicory quarters in it. Mix together the pesto and olive oil and brush over the leaves. Season with salt and pepper. Cover with foil and bake in a preheated oven, 180°C/350°F/Gas Mark 4, for 10 minutes. Remove the foil and bake for a further 10 minutes.

2. Take the dish out of the oven and sprinkle the leaves with the Emmental and nutmeg. Put the dish back in the oven and bake for 10–20 minutes, or until cheese has melted and is bubbling. Serve immediately.

Chicken and Roquefort Caesar Salad

Serves 1
Carbs 4g
Fat 45g
Protein 37g

1 boneless, skinless
chicken breast

150g (5oz) shredded cos
lettuce

25g (1oz) crumbled
Roquefort cheese

Garlic marinade

½ tablespoon olive oil

½ garlic clove, chopped

1 teaspoon chopped parsley

½ teaspoon grated
lemon rind

salt and pepper

Caesar dressing

1 tablespoon Mayonnaise
(see below)

½ teaspoon Dijon mustard

splash of Worcestershire
sauce

½ garlic clove

1 tablespoon fresh
lemon juice

1–2 anchovy fillets, rinsed
and patted dry

1 teaspoon olive oil

salt and pepper

1. In a medium bowl, whisk together all the ingredients for the marinade. Put the chicken in the marinade and turn to coat it on all over. Set aside.
2. To make the dressing, combine the mayonnaise, mustard, Worcestershire sauce, garlic, lemon juice and anchovies in a food processor or blender, processing until smooth. With the motor running, gradually drizzle the oil into the dressing. Season with salt and pepper, then aside until needed.
3. Put the chicken on a rack below a preheated grill and cook for 4 minutes on each side, until firm and cooked through. Transfer the cooked chicken to a chopping board and slice into long, thin pieces.
4. Toss the lettuce with the dressing until evenly coated. Sprinkle with the cheese and toss again. Top with the chicken slices and serve.

Mayonnaise

Per tablespoon:
Carbs 0.5g
Fat 13.6g
Protein 0.5g

2 large egg yolks

275ml (9 fl oz) extra virgin
olive oil (or ¾ olive oil
and ¼ flaxseed oil)

2 tablespoons cider vinegar

2 tablespoons lemon juice

½ teaspoon mustard powder

sea salt and pepper

1. Put the egg yolks in a food processor or blender and begin blending on a very low setting. Very gradually add some oil, a couple of drops at a time. When the mixture resembles a light emulsion, pour in the oil in a slow, steady stream until you have added half of it.
2. Add the vinegar, lemon juice, mustard powder and salt and pepper while continuing to blend slowly. Gradually add the remaining oil. Taste and adjust the seasoning.

Chicken Ratatouille

2 tablespoons olive oil

2 x 150g (5oz) chicken breasts, skinned, boned and cut in 2.5cm (1in) pieces

60g (2¼oz) thinly sliced courgettes

75g (2½oz) cubed aubergine

150g (5oz) thinly sliced onion

50g (2oz) sliced green pepper

75g (2½oz) sliced mushrooms

400g (13oz) can tomatoes

2 garlic cloves, finely chopped

1 teaspoon organic vegetable boullion powder

1 teaspoon crushed dried sweet basil

1 teaspoon dried parsley

½ teaspoon black pepper

Serves 2
Carbs 17g
Fat 17g
Protein 42g

1. Heat the oil in a large frying pan, add the chicken and sauté, stirring, for about 2 minutes. Add the courgettes, aubergine, onion, green pepper and mushrooms. Cook, stirring occasionally, for about 15 minutes, or until tender.

2. Add the tomatoes to the pan, stirring carefully. Stir in the garlic, vegetable stock powder, basil, parsley and pepper and simmer, uncovered, for about 5 minutes, or until a fork goes easily into the chicken.

Crunchy Rice Salad

Serves 1
Carbs 30g
Fat 14g
Protein 11g

90g (3oz) finely chopped broccoli

90g (3oz) finely chopped courgettes

90g (3oz) finely chopped mixed red and yellow peppers

25g (1oz) finely chopped spring onion

40g (1½oz) finely sliced mushrooms

2 tablespoons pesto sauce

50g (2oz) cooked brown rice

50g (2oz) cooked wild rice

salt and pepper

To garnish:

Parmesan shavings

basil leaves

1. Put all the vegetables into a large hot frying pan or wok and add about 2 tablespoons of water. Cook for 3–5 minutes, until the vegetables have softened. Reduce the heat to medium, add the pesto sauce and stir until all the vegetables are covered.

2. Throw in the cooked rice and stir the mixture thoroughly. Raise the heat for 1 minute, tossing the vegetables and rice together until the rice has warmed through.

3. Season with salt and pepper and serve garnished with a few Parmesan shavings and some basil leaves. This dish is also great cold as a salad.

NOTE

By keeping the ratio of low GI vegetables higher than that of the high GI rice, this rice salad becomes a healthy dish that won't send blood-sugar levels soaring. The fact that the vegetables are only lightly cooked helps them to retain their all-important fibre and many of their nutrients.

Sweet Potato and Cauliflower Purée

75g (2½oz) peeled and cubed sweet potato

90g (3oz) roughly chopped cauliflower

1 teaspoon organic vegetable boullion powder

black pepper

ground nutmeg

Serves 1
Carbs 20g
Fat 2.7g
Protein 6.7g

1. Put the sweet potato and cauliflower into a saucepan of hot water and bring to the boil then simmer, covered, for 6–7 minutes, or until the sweet potato is tender.
2. Transfer the vegetables to a food processor or blender, add the stock powder and process until smooth. Season to taste with pepper and nutmeg.

Spicy Roasted Aubergine with Tofu

Serves 1
Carbs 4.7g
Fat 9g
Protein 8

1. Heat a frying pan or wok until hot, add the aubergine and cook until the skin begins to char, turning it to cook on all sides. Remove from the heat and allow cool, then cut the aubergine diagonally into 1cm (½in) strips.
2. Using a food processor or blender, blend the chilli, garlic, coriander root, onion, lime juice and fish sauce until smooth.
3. Heat the oil in a wok or pan and add the spice paste, stirring it over a high heat for 1 minute or until fragrant. Add the aubergine strips and cook for 3 minutes. Add the tofu and half of the basil and gently stir through.
4. Serve the aubergine garnished with the remaining basil and the dried shrimp, if you like.

1 small aubergine

1 small red chilli

1 garlic clove, crushed

1 coriander root, chopped

1 tablespoon chopped onion

1 tablespoon lime juice

½ tablespoon Thai fish sauce

½ tablespoon coconut oil

50g (2oz) firm cubed tofu

1 tablespoon chopped Thai or sweet basil

½ teaspoon finely chopped dried shrimp, to garnish (optional)

TIP

This dish is also great cold, so make double the quantity and have some for lunch the next day.

Moroccan Lamb with Orange and Chickpeas

Serves 8
Carbs 18g
Fat 19g
Protein 31g

1. Drain the chickpeas and rinse under cold water. Put them in a large saucepan, cover with water and bring to the boil, then reduce the heat and simmer, covered, for about 1–1½ hours until tender. Remove the pan from the heat and add a little salt. Set aside.

2. In a large bowl, combine half of the olive oil with the cumin, cinnamon, ginger, turmeric and saffron, plus ½ teaspoon of salt and ½ teaspoon of pepper. Add the cubed lamb, toss and set aside for 20 minutes.

3. Heat the remaining oil in a large heavy-based pan and fry the lamb in batches until well browned. Using a slotted spoon, transfer the meat to a large flameproof casserole.

4. Add the onions to the pan and stir constantly until browned. Stir in the garlic and the tomatoes with the measured water, stirring and scraping the base of the pan. Pour the onion and tomato mixture into the casserole and add enough water to just cover the lamb. Bring to the boil over a high heat and skim off any surface foam. Lower the heat and simmer for about 1 hour, or until the meat is tender.

5. Drain the chickpeas and reserve the liquid. Add the chickpeas with about 1 cup of their cooking liquid to the lamb and simmer for 30 minutes.

6. Stir in the olives, lemon and orange rind and simmer for a final 30 minutes.

7. Stir in half of the chopped coriander then serve garnished with the remaining coriander and with a crisp green salad or Spicy Cauliflower (see page 76). When cool, this dish may be frozen in a plastic container.

225g (7½oz) chickpeas, soaked in cold water overnight

4 tablespoons olive oil

2 teaspoons ground cumin

1 teaspoon ground cinnamon

1 teaspoon ground ginger

1 teaspoon ground turmeric

½ teaspoon powdered saffron

1.5 kg (3lb) shoulder of lamb, trimmed of all fat and cut into 5cm (2in) cubes

2 onions, roughly chopped

3 garlic cloves, finely chopped

2 tomatoes, skinned, deseeded and chopped

250ml (8fl oz) cold water

12 pitted black olives, sliced

grated rind of 1 unwaxed lemon

grated rind of 1 unwaxed orange or 1 tablespoon dried orange rind

6 tablespoons chopped coriander leaves

salt and pepper

Baked Courgettes with Goats' Cheese and Mint

4 small courgettes

1 tablespoon olive oil

50g (2oz) goats' cheese, cut into thin strips

small bunch of mint, finely chopped

black pepper

Serves 1
Carbs 10g
Fat 23g
Protein 10g

1. Cut out 4 rectangles of foil, each large enough to enclose 1 courgette. Brush each rectangle on one side with a little olive oil.

2. Top and tail the courgettes, then cut a thin slit along the centre of each one.
Insert the goats' cheese into the slits, add a little mint and sprinkle with oil and pepper.

3. Wrap each courgette in a piece of foil and place on a baking tray. Bake in a preheated oven, 180°C/350°F/Gas Mark 4, for about 25 minutes; or 20 minutes and then brown under a hot grill.

Steamed Mussels with Lemongrass, Basil and Wine

Serves 4
Carbs 5g
Fat 5g
Protein 12g

1. Discard any open mussels. Scrub the outside of the remaining mussels with a brush. Remove and throw away the beards. Soak the mussels in a bowl of cold water for 10 minutes, then drain.

2. Heat the oil in a wok. Add the onion, garlic, lemongrass and chilli and cook for 4 minutes over a low heat. Stir in the wine and fish sauce and cook for a further 3 minutes.

3. Add the mussels to the wok and toss well. Cover the wok and increase the heat, then cook for 3–4 minutes, or until the mussels open. Do not overcook, or the mussels will become tough. Discard any that still haven't opened, add the basil and serve immediately.

1kg (2lb) fresh small black mussels

1 tablespoon coconut oil

1 onion, finely chopped

4 garlic cloves, finely chopped

2 lemongrass stems, white part only, finely chopped

1–2 teaspoons chopped red chilli

250ml (8fl oz) white wine

1 tablespoon Thai fish sauce

75g (2½oz) chopped Thai or sweet basil

Creamy Cucumber Salsa

2 medium cucumbers

250ml (8fl oz) soured cream

250ml (8fl oz) plain yogurt

1 tablespoon chopped parsley

1 tablespoon chopped coriander leaves

1 teaspoon ground cumin

salt and pepper

Serves 8
Carbs 4g
Fat 6g
Protein 2.8g

1. Peel, deseed and shred the cucumbers. Put the shredded cucumber in a bowl with the soured cream, yogurt, parsley, coriander and cumin. Season with salt and pepper to taste and mix well. Cover and chill for at least 2 hours.

TIP

Serve this salsa chilled with lamb, sardines or tuna.

Curbing the carb on a vegetarian diet

Adapting the Fast Track, No Backtracking and Keep on Tracking plans for vegetarians raises all sorts of issues. It certainly isn't impossible, but your level of choice will be somewhat restricted in the initial phases of the plan – especially if you are a *bona fide* vegetarian who doesn't eat fish or eggs, as well as meat. A balanced healthy diet is the ultimate aim of these plans.

Many people adopt a vegetarian diet for reasons of health rather than ethics, but unless you are careful about menu-planning, the average vegetarian diet isn't necessarily any healthier or less fattening than that of a non-vegetarian. There is often a tendency to combine too many complex carbohydrates with high levels of saturated fats – think pizza, jacket potato and cheese, fries with manufactured mayonnaise or sugar–ridden ketchup. In fact the chances are your diet could be less healthy. This is because vegetarians need to eat a variety of plant-based foods to provide all the essential amino acids that are readily available in animal protein. If just one of the essential amino acids is low or missing then protein synthesis will fall to a very low level or stop altogether.

As well as being a vital source of protein for vegetarians, nuts are rich in vitamin E and magnesium.

Complimentary proteins

The key to ensuring that you recive the full compliment of essential amino acids on a vegetarian diet is to combine beans and grains. If you always choose a protein and a grain from the two lists below then your protein intake should be balanced.

Proteins	Grains
Almonds	Brown rice
Black eyed peas	Bulgur wheat
Chick peas	Corn
Green peas	Couscous
Kidney beans	Sesame seeds
Lentils	Wholegrain or rye bread
Lima beans	Whole wheat pasta
Peanuts	
White beans	

The risks of a diet too low in protein

If you are not careful then you may not have enough protein in your diet. Protein deficiencies in adults may result in lack of vigour and stamina, mental depression, weakness and poor resistance to infection. Antibodies will not function as well as they could – a condition that impairs the healing of wounds and recovery from disease. If you have been through a period of ill health then a higher intake of protein is vital in order to rebuild or replace tissues that are no longer functioning properly.

Good nutrition

In addition to making sure that you eat enough protein, a vegetarian diet may also be lacking in iron, zinc, calcium and vitamin B_{12} and D – all of which are normally found in animal products. However, these vitamins and minerals can all be found in alternative animal-free sources, and these foods should be staple foods on a vegetarian diet (see right).

Low-carb plans for vegetarians

You may think that it is impossible to follow the Fast Track, No Backtracking and Keep on Tracking plans if you are vegetarian, but you would be wrong. If you want to create vegetarian versions of these plans then there are a number of simple rules that you will find it helpful to follow:

◆ Eradicate all processed and refined carbohydrates from your diet.
◆ Follow all the general guidelines for the individual diet plans, such as drinking lots of water and eating the bulk of your fruits and vegetables raw.
◆ Use the individual plans as a starting point and adapt the recipes to suit your diet (see page 108).
◆ Use tofu, whey protein drinks (see page 60), certain cheeses, eggs and nuts to provide adequate levels of protein and help you to balance your blood sugar levels.
◆ Always carry snacks such as nuts, protein drinks or hard-boiled eggs with you as it may sometimes be difficult to stick to your diet when you are eating out.
◆ Try to avoid situations where it would be very easy to break your resolve, such as when you are hungry and the only lunch option available is a sandwich.
◆ If a book exists called *A million and one things to do with tofu* – buy it.
◆ Make food as interesting as possible by experimenting with fresh herbs, spices and oils rich in omega-3 fatty acids such as flaxseed oil.
◆ Boost the nutritional value of your food by adding fresh sprouts, such as alfalfa, to your salads, soups and smoothies.
◆ If you start to feel tired and lacking in energy, add small amounts of brown rice or other wholegrains to your meals.

VEGETARIAN SOURCES FOR ESSENTIAL VITAMINS AND MINERALS

Iron
Cashews, tomato juice, rice, tofu, lentils, chickpeas

Calcium
Dairy products, fortified soya milk, fortified orange juice, tofu, kale, broccoli.

Vitamin D
Fortified milk and soya milk

Vitamin B_{12}
Eggs, dairy products, fortified soya milk, cereals, miso

Zinc
Whole grains, eggs, dairy products, nuts, tofu, leafy vegetables (spinach, lettuce, cabbage), onions, potatoes, carrots, celery, radishes

Adapting the recipe plans for vegetarians

It is easy to adapt all of the recipes and meal plans in this book. Here are some simple suggestions for making the recipes vegetarian:

◆ Replace the meat or fish in a recipe with Portobello mushrooms or aubergine, but remember that this will raise the carbohydrate levels in the recipe. You will also need to take extra whey-protein drinks and maybe increase your intake of nuts and high protein snacks to keep your protein levels high enough.

◆ Cook with tofu instead of the meat or fish. However, tofu has a quarter as much protein per gram as meat and a third as much as most fish. This means that not only should you replace the meat or fish in a recipe with a higher amount of tofu, but you should also add whey-protein powder to the recipe or supplement your meal with a whey-protein shake.

◆ If you eat fish, simply replace the meat elements of a recipe with a fish equivalent. Most of the recipes can easily be adapted in this way.

◆ If you don't eat fish, then be vigilant about taking 2 teaspoons of flaxseed oil a day to ensure you are getting sufficient omega-3 essential fatty acids.

◆ Add some whey-protein powder to sauces and soups as a means of increasing their nutritional value.

Tofu is very versatile. Use silken tofu in soups and firm tofu in place of meat and fish.

Fast Track

The Fast Track plan is the most difficult to adapt for vegetarians because there are so many vegetarian staples that are restricted or not allowed. Once you move on to the other plans you can start to reintroduce a lot of these foods and things should become easier.

When you adapt Fast Track for a vegetarian diet, it is important that you plan to eat plenty of cashew nuts, tofu, dairy products, fortified soya milk, kale, broccoli, eggs, leafy vegetables, celery and radishes to ensure that you are getting a full compliment of vitamins and minerals.

It is also very important that you eat the right amount of protein. Here are some suggestions for eating around 150g protein daily on vegetarian version of the fast track plan:

◆ 2-egg omelette with 15g (½oz)of whey-protein powder added to the mixture = 26g protein

◆ 200g (7oz) cottage cheese = 26g protein

◆ 125g (4oz) feta cheese salad = 23g protein

◆ Whey-protein shake = 20g protein

◆ 25g (1oz) walnuts 7g protein

◆ 25g (1oz) sunflower seeds = 6.5g protein

◆ Whey protein drink = 20g protein

◆ 150g (5oz) tofu = 12g protein

◆ daily allowance of 250ml (8 fl oz) milk = 8g protein

GOOD PROTEIN SOURCES FOR

VEGETARIANS ON FAST TRACK

Whey-protein powder

Dairy products

Eggs

Roasted pumpkin and squash seeds

Soya Flour

Raw, firm tofu

Blanched almonds

Keep on Tracking

When you move on to the Keep on Tracking it would also be wise to continue having whey-protein drinks on a daily basis to ensure that you are maintaining a reasonable level of high Biological Value protein in your diet. Three protein drinks per day would ensure around 60 grams of high quality protein per day. Alternatively, you could incorporate whey-protein powder into sauces and soups to increase their nutritional value.

These foods should be gradually re-introduced during Keep on Tracking:

◆ Oats
◆ Lentils, cooked
◆ Rice, brown, long grain
◆ Chickpeas, cooked
◆ Wild rice
◆ Wholegrains

No Backtracking

Don't fall back into your old eating habits. The following tips will help you to make these choices when planning your diet in the future.

◆ Eat rye bread or wholegrain bread rather than white bread.
◆ Try eating chickpeas, soya beans, pulses, brown rice or wild rice.
◆ Choose wholewheat pasta rather than pasta made from refined flour.
◆ Eat plenty of raw fibrous vegetables, instead of relying on cooked dense vegetables such as carrots.
◆ Moderate your intake of potatoes.
◆ Eat enough protein – supplement your diet with whey protein drinks if you need to.
◆ Make sure that you are getting sufficient omega-3 fatty acids in your diet.

Cooked potatoes have a very high GI and will send your blood sugar soaring.

Vegetarian Q&A

Q.I have a job which involves a lot of socialising and business lunches, and because I am a vegetarian, sometimes the choice is pretty limited. I really do think it's going to be impossible for me to stick to this way of eating, and I don't want to draw attention to the fact that I am dieting.

A. Try to ensure that you book the restaurants for business lunches, that way you can try to eat at places that serve a good range of vegetarian food. Most chefs are happy to whip up a mushroom omelette, and ordering a salad shouldn't be a problem. Try a plate of olives and crudites instead of hitting the bread basket and if you are facing a carb laden buffet, have a whey protein shake before you arrive so that you aren't tempted to snack.

Protein Pancakes

Serves 1
Carbs 4.6g
Fat 17g
Protein 15g

1. Separate the eggs and beat the whites until stiff.
2. Combine the yolks with the cottage cheese, soda water, soya flour, salt and baking powder. Gently fold in the egg whites until the mixture is thoroughly blended.
3. Heat the coconut oil in a frying pan. Spoon in dollops of the mixture and cook until the underside is golden brown. Flip the pancakes over and take the pan off the heat. Serve immediately.

TIP

These pancakes can be served however you like. Good accompaniments are ½ cup chopped strawberries and a tablespoon of soured cream, or crispy bacon, or simply sprinkle them with cinnamon.

2 eggs

50g (2oz) cottage cheese

1 teaspoon soda water

15g (½oz) soya flour

pinch of salt

½ teaspoon baking powder

1 tablespoon coconut oil

Spinach and Cheese Omelette

2 eggs

1–2 teaspoons olive oil

90g (3½oz) raw baby
spinach, chopped

25g (1oz) cheese of your
choice, such as mozzarella,
ricotta, Cheddar, grated or
crumbled

dash of Tabasco sauce
(optional)

salt and pepper

Serves 1
Carbs 2.1g
Fat 26g
Protein 21g

1. Beat the eggs and season to taste with salt and pepper.
2. Heat the oil in a frying pan and add the egg mixture.
3. When the egg has set completely, scatter the spinach over it and top with the cheese and a dash of Tabasco, if required. Fold the omelette over, lift it carefully out of the pan and serve immediately.

Chickpea and Parsley Soup

250g (9oz) chickpeas, soaked overnight

1 small onion

3 garlic cloves

40g (1½oz) parsley

2 tablespoons olive oil

1.2 litres (2 pints) vegetable stock

juice and grated rind of ½ lemon

salt and pepper

Serves 6
Carbs 20g
Fat 7.3g
Protein 9g

1. Drain the chickpeas and rinse under cold water. Put them in a saucepan of fresh water. Bring to the boil, then simmer for 1–1½ hours, until just tender.

2. Put the onion, garlic and parsley in a food processor or blender and blend until finely chopped.

3. Heat the oil in a saucepan and cook the onion mixture over a low heat until slightly softened. Add the chickpeas and cook gently for 1–2 minutes.

4. Add the stock, season well with salt and pepper and bring to the boil. Cover and cook for 20 minutes, or until the chickpeas are really tender.

5. Allow the soup to cool for a while, then part-purée it in a food processor or blender, or mash it with a fork, so that it retains plenty of texture.

6. Pour the soup into a clean pan, add the lemon juice and adjust the seasoning as necessary, and heat through. Serve the soup topped with grated lemon rind and cracked black pepper. When cool, any unused portions may be stored in a plastic container and frozen.

Salade Tricolore

½ avocado, peeled and thinly sliced

75g (2½oz) thinly sliced mozzarella cheese

1 large tomato, thinly sliced

1 tablespoon lemon juice

1 tablespoon Pesto Sauce (see page 118)

salt and pepper

basil leaves, to garnish

Serves 1
Carbs 6.3g
Fat 27g
Protein 49g

1. Arrange the avocado, mozzarella and tomato slices on a large plate.

2. Mix together the lemon juice and pesto and drizzle over the salad. Season with salt and pepper and leave for 5–10 minutes to allow the flavours to blend. Scatter with basil leaves and serve.

Energy-Booster Soup

Serves 4
Carbs 9.6g
Fat 4.4g
Protein 39g

1. Heat the oil in a large heavy-based saucepan and sauté the onion and garlic for 5 minutes.

2. Add the stock, spring onions, tomatoes, watercress, basil and pumpkin, season with salt and pepper then cover and simmer for 1 hour.

3. To serve the soup, add 2 scoops of whey-protein powder to each serving. When cool, any unused portions may be stored in a plastic container and frozen.

1 tablespoon olive oil

1 red onion, chopped

2 garlic cloves, crushed

1 litre (1¾ pints) vegetable stock

2 spring onions, chopped

400g (13oz) can chopped Italian tomatoes

75g (2½oz) chopped watercress

75g (2½oz) chopped basil

225g (7½oz) chopped pumpkin

salt and pepper

8 scoops micro-filtered whey-protein powder, to serve

Hot Haloumi with Fattoush Salad

Serves 1
Carbs 7g
Fat 42g
Protein 30g

1 teaspoon olive oil

125g (4oz) haloumi cheese, thickly sliced

Fattoush salad

40g (1½oz) finely sliced red pepper

40g (1½oz) finely sliced yellow pepper

40g (1½oz) chopped cucumber

40g (1½oz) finely chopped spring onions

1 tablespoon chopped flat leaf parsley

1 tablespoon chopped mint

1 tablespoon chopped coriander leaves

Dressing

½ teaspoon crushed garlic

1 tablespoon olive oil or flaxseed oil

juice of ½ lemon

salt and pepper

1. Lightly oil a frying pan with olive oil and heat through. Put the haloumi in the pan and fry over a medium to high heat for 1–2 minutes on each side until golden brown. Keep warm.
2. Put the red and yellow peppers, cucumber, spring onions, parsley, mint and coriander in a bowl.
3. To make the dressing, mix the garlic with the oil and lemon juice and season with salt and pepper to taste.
4. Pour the dressing over the salad and toss lightly to mix. Serve with the warm haloumi.

Baba Ghanoush

Serves 6
Carbs 1.3g
Fat 15g
Protein 3.8g

1. Place the aubergines on a foil-lined rack about 10cm (4in) below a preheated hot grill; turn them frequently, until the skin has blackened and blistered. Remove the skin, chop the flesh roughly and leave it to drain in a colander, squeezing out as much liquid from the aubergines as possible.

2. Put the flesh in a food processor or blender, then add the garlic, tahini, almonds, lemon juice and cumin and season with salt and pepper. Blend for several seconds. Roughly chop half the mint and stir it into the dip.

3. Spoon the dip into a bowl, scatter with the remaining mint leaves and drizzle with the olive oil.

2 small aubergines

1 garlic clove, crushed

4 tablespoons tahini paste

25g (1oz) ground almonds

juice of ½ lemon

½ teaspoon ground cumin

2 tablespoons mint leaves

2 tablespoons olive oil

salt and pepper

Stuffed Mushrooms with Tofu, Basil and Pine Nuts

Serves 1
Carbs 6g
Fat 40g
Protein 26g

300ml (½ pint) boiling water

1 teaspoon organic vegetable boullion powder

2 large Portobello mushrooms, stalks removed

1 tablespoon olive oil

40g (1½oz) finely chopped red onion

125g (4oz) finely cubed tofu

1 tablespoon pine nuts, dry-fried in a hot pan until golden brown

¼ teaspoon cayenne pepper

1 tablespoon chopped basil

25g (1oz) finely grated Parmesan cheese

75g (2½oz) baby spinach leaves

salt and pepper

1. Pour the boiling water into a wide pan, then stir in the stock powder. Add the mushrooms and poach for 2–3 minutes then remove and drain on kitchen paper.

2. Heat a little of the oil and gently fry the onion until soft. Remove from the heat and allow to cool.

3. Mix the onion, tofu, pine nuts, cayenne pepper, basil and the remaining oil. Season well with salt and pepper.

4. Sprinkle some grated cheese over each mushroom, then stuff the onion mixture into the mushrooms. Place them in a flameproof dish about 15cm (6in) below a preheated medium grill for about 10 minutes, until heated through and the cheese has melted.

5. To serve, scatter the spinach leaves on a plate and arrange the hot mushrooms on top (the heat of the mushrooms will wilt the spinach), with a generous dollop of Baba Ghanoush (see opposite) on the side, if you like.

Wasabi and Ginger Tofu with Crunchy Alfalfa Salad

100g (3½oz) firm tofu

½ teaspoon olive oil for frying

Wasabi and ginger marinade

1 teaspoon extra virgin olive oil

1 tablespoon tamari or soy sauce

1 garlic clove, crushed

2.5cm (1in) piece of ginger, finely grated

1 teaspoon lemon juice

½ teaspoon wasabi paste

Alfalfa salad

75g (2½oz) shredded cos lettuce

1 small tomato, sliced

2 teaspoons finely chopped spring onion

1 garlic clove, crushed

½ avocado, sliced

½ fennel bulb, finely sliced

25g (1oz) alfalfa sprouts or bean sprouts

25g (1oz) sunflower seeds

1 tablespoon olive oil

1 tablespoon lime juice

salt and pepper

Serves 1
Carbs 18.4g
Fat 59g
Protein 22g

1. Slice the tofu into long thin strips, then place them in a shallow dish.

2. To make the marinade, mix together the olive oil, tamari, garlic, ginger, lemon juice and wasabi and pour it over the tofu. Leave to marinate for as long as you can (overnight if possible).

3. To make the salad, put the lettuce, tomato, spring onion, garlic, avocado, fennel and alfalfa or bean sprouts in a bowl. Add the sunflower seeds, olive or flaxseed oil and lime juice. Season with salt and pepper and toss well.

4. Heat a heavy-based frying pan or a griddle pan and add small amount of oil. Fry the tofu strips until golden brown on both sides. Serve with the alfalfa salad.

Protein-Packed Cauliflower Jacket

1 large baking potato

250g (9oz) chopped cauliflower, lightly steamed for 10 minutes

125g (4oz) silken tofu

1 tablespoon flaxseed oil

1 spring onion, finely chopped

1 tablespoon chopped chives

1 teaspoon organic vegetable bouillon powder

25g (1oz) crumbled or grated feta or Parmesan cheese (optional)

black pepper

Serves 1
Carbs 10g
Fat 25g
Protein 17g

1. Scrub the potato and prick the skin with a fork. Bake in a preheated oven, 200°C/400°F/Gas Mark 6, for 1 hour, until the inside is soft and the outside crisp. Allow to cool slightly.

2. Put the cauliflower in a large bowl and mash with a potato masher. Add the tofu and oil and mix thoroughly until the mixture looks like mashed potato.
Add the spring onion, chives and bouillon powder and stir well, with salt and pepper to taste.

3. Scoop the flesh out of the potato skin and discard. Refill the skin with the tofu and cauliflower mixture. If you like, sprinkle it with crumbled or grated cheese then return it to the hot oven for 10–15 minutes until it is heated right through and the cheese is bubbling.

4. Serve with a cup of steamed broccoli or some other vegetable from the permitted list.

Hummus

150g (5oz) dried chickpeas, or 2 x 425g (14oz) cans chickpeas, thoroughly drained

juice of 2 lemons

2 garlic cloves, sliced

2 tablespoons olive oil

pinch of cayenne pepper

200g (7oz) tahini paste salt and pepper

To garnish
extra virgin olive oil

cayenne pepper

1 tablespoon flat leaf parsley

Serves 6
Carbs 13g
Fat 25g
Protein 11g

1. If using dried chickpeas, put them in a bowl and cover with plenty of water. Leave them to soak overnight.

2. Drain the chickpeas and cover with fresh water in a saucepan. Bring to the boil, then reduce the heat and simmer gently for 1–1½ hours, or until soft. Drain thoroughly.

3. Put the chickpeas in a food processor or blender and work to a smooth purée. Add the lemon juice, garlic, olive oil, cayenne pepper and tahini and blend again until creamy.

4. Season with salt and pepper and transfer to a serving dish. To serve, drizzle with oil and sprinkle with cayenne pepper and parsley sprigs.

Guacamole

1 avocado

juice of ½ lime

½ garlic clove, finely chopped

1 tablespoon finely chopped onion

1 small tomato, diced

1 tablespoon chopped coriander leaves

½ teaspoon finely chopped red chilli pepper

generous pinch of cumin powder

pinch of mild chilli powder

salt

Serves 1
Carbs 3.5
Fat 19g
Protein 2g

1. Cut the avocado in half and scoop out the flesh. Roughly mash the flesh with a fork and stir in the lime juice. Gradually add the garlic, onion, tomato, coriander and chilli pepper, mix them in well and season with cumin, chilli powder and salt.

2. Serve with grilled chicken, homemade burgers, potato skins or crudités.

Pesto Sauce

Serves 16
Carbs 1g
Fat 42g
Protein 3g

1. Put the oil, garlic, basil and pine nuts in a food processor or blender and blend until you reach the desired consistency. Add the Parmesan and stir until evenly distributed. Cover and keep refrigerated until required.

TIP
Blend 1–2 tablespoons pesto with an equal amount of vegetable or chicken stock for a quick marinade or dressing. Put 1 tablespoon into a carton of natural yogurt for a great dip.

450ml (¾ pint) olive oil (or 300ml (½ pint) olive oil and 150ml (¼ pint) flaxseed oil)

5 garlic cloves, roughly chopped

3 cups chopped basil

75g (2½oz) pine nuts

75g (2½oz) finely grated Parmesan cheese

Grilled Aubergine Parcels with Tomato Dressing and Pine Nuts

1 long, large aubergine

125g (4oz) mozzarella cheese

1 large or 2 small plum tomatoes

8 large basil leaves

1 tablespoon olive oil

1 tablespoon pine nuts, dry-fried in a hot pan until golden brown

torn basil leaves

salt and pepper

Tomato dressing

2 tablespoons olive oil or flaxseed oil

1 teaspoon balsamic vinegar

1 teaspoon sun-dried tomato paste

1 teaspoon lemon juice

Serves 2
Carbs 6g
Fat 37g
Protein 17g

1. Remove the stalk from the aubergine and cut it thinly lengthwise – you need 8 slices in total, disregarding the 2 outer edges. Put the aubergine slices in a pan of boiling salted water and cook for 2 minutes, then drain and dry on kitchen paper. Cut the mozzarella into 4 slices and the tomato into 8 slices, again disregarding the outer edges.

2. Take two aubergine slices and put them in a flameproof dish, forming a cross. Place a slice of tomato on top, season with salt and pepper, add a basil leaf, a slice of mozzarella, another basil leaf, then more salt and pepper, and finally another slice of tomato. Fold the edges of the aubergine around the filling to make a parcel. Repeat with the other ingredients to make 4 parcels in total. Cover and chill in the refrigerator for 20 minutes.

3. To make the dressing, whisk together the oil, vinegar, tomato paste and lemon juice and set aside.

4. Brush the aubergine parcels with olive oil. Place the dish under a preheated grill and cook for about 5 minutes on each side, until golden brown. Serve hot, drizzled with the dressing and scattered with the pine nuts and torn basil leaves.

Sauces, salsas & marinades

Hollandaise Sauce

100g (3½oz) butter

4 egg yolks, beaten

juice of 1 lemon

1 teaspoon Dijon mustard

salt and pepper

Serves 2
Carbs 0.4g
Fat 51g
Protein 6g

1. Melt one-third of the butter in a bain-marie, then remove from the heat.
2. Beat the egg yolks in a bowl, using either a hand-held electric beater or a whisk. Slowly add the melted butter, stirring continually.
3. Return the mixture to the bain-marie over simmering water and continue to add little knobs of butter, whisking all the time.
4. Once all the butter has melted and integrated, take the bain-marie off the heat and stir in the lemon juice and mustard and season with salt and pepper.

TIP
Serve with grilled chicken breast and steamed asparagus.

Salsa Verde

Serves 4
Carbs 0.3g
Fat 28g
Protein 0.3g

25g (1oz) finely chopped parsley

2 garlic cloves, very finely chopped

2 tablespoons capers, rinsed and chopped

125ml (4fl oz) extra virgin olive oil

1 tablespoon red wine vinegar or lemon juice

salt and pepper

1. Combine the parsley, garlic, capers and olive oil in a bowl, then stir in the vinegar or lemon juice to taste. Season with salt and pepper.

TIP
For variety, include a small portion of other herbs, such as chervil, basil, dill, fennel, thyme or rocket, with the parsley. If you're using lemon juice, not vinegar, add some of the lemon rind to the sauce. This salsa is particularly good with fish.

Watermelon and Green Peppercorn Salsa

2 tablespoons finely chopped red onion

400g (13oz) deseeded and finely cubed watermelon

2 tablespoons lime juice

2 tablespoons green peppercorns, rinsed

salt and cayenne pepper

Serves 4
Carbs 6.5g
Fat 0g
Protein 0.5g

1. Cover the onion with cold water, then leave for 10 minutes to reduce some of the acidity. Drain the onion and pat dry on kitchen paper.
2. Combine the watermelon with the onion, 1 tablespoon of the lime juice, the peppercorns, salt and cayenne pepper. Cover and chill for about 1 hour.
3. Just before serving, stir in the remaining tablespoon of lime juice.

Roasted Tomato and Mint Salsa

Serves 3
Carbs 5.4g
Fat 4.5g
Protein 1.8g

3 large plum tomatoes, with the tops removed

1 garlic clove, finely chopped

1 tablespoon lime juice

1 tablespoon extra virgin olive oil

100g (3½oz) finely chopped red peppers

1 tablespoon finely chopped coriander leaves

1 tablespoon finely chopped mint

generous pinch of lime rind

generous pinch of orange rind

salt and pepper

1. Put the tomatoes in a heavy-based pan and cook over a medium to high heat until they are blackened all over.
2. While the tomatoes are still warm, put them in a food processor or blender with the garlic and chop roughly. Transfer to a bowl and allow to cool to room temperature.
3. Add the lime juice, oil, red peppers, coriander, mint and lime and orange rind and season to taste with salt and pepper. Mix well and leave to stand for at least 30 minutes before serving.

TIP
Serve this salsa with lamb, white fish such as cod, chicken, beefburgers or steak.

Cucumber and Mint Salsa

1 cucumber

2 tablespoons dark walnut oil

2 tablespoons fresh lemon juice

1 tablespoon finely chopped mint

1 tablespoon salt

Serves 4
Carbs 1g
Fat 7g
Protein trace

1. Peel the cucumber and cut it in half lengthwise. Scoop out and discard the seeds. Finely chop the flesh and put it in a colander. Sprinkle the cucumber with salt, then place the colander over a plate for 30 minutes to catch the water.

2. Rinse the cucumber and squeeze out any excess moisture. Put the cucumber in a mixing bowl and add the oil, lemon juice and mint. Season to taste with salt and pepper. Mix well and pour into a small serving bowl.

Avocado Salsa

2 teaspoons olive oil

1 shallot, finely chopped

2 teaspoons raspberry vinegar

1 teaspoon poppy seeds

½ large avocado, peeled, pitted and cut into 1cm (½in) cubes

125g (4oz) cup fresh raspberries

½ red chilli pepper, deseeded and finely chopped

Serves 2
Carbs 6g
Fat 37g
Protein 4g

1. Heat the oil in a small saucepan over a medium to high heat. Add the shallot and sauté for 1 minute, stirring frequently. Lower the heat to medium, add the vinegar and poppy seeds and cook for 2 minutes, stirring constantly. Remove the pan from the heat and allow to cool.

2. Combine the avocado, raspberries and chilli. Add the vinegar mixture and fold in gently to coat the avocado. Serve immediately.

TIP

This salsa is ideal with chicken, venison and turkey. It will not keep. Don't use the thinner-skinned green avocados as they will react with the raspberries and spoil the salsa.

Quick Coconut Curry Sauce

75g (3oz) chopped onion

3 garlic cloves, crushed

1 tablespoon coconut oil

400g (13oz) can coconut milk

2 teaspoons hot, medium or mild curry powder, according to taste

pinch of turmeric

salt and pepper

Serves 4
Carbs 8.2g
Fat 4.2g
Protein 1g

1. Put the onion and garlic in a saucepan with the coconut oil and fry over a medium heat until browned. Add the coconut milk, curry powder and turmeric and simmer for 2–3 minutes. Season with salt and pepper then pour the sauce over the dish of your choice.

Simple Marinade for Chicken, Fish and Tofu

juice of ½ lemon

1 tablespoon olive oil

1 garlic clove, crushed

1 teaspoon dried thyme

salt and pepper

Makes enough for a 125–75g (4–6oz) portion of chicken, fish or tofu
Carbs 2g
Fat 14g
Protein trace

1. Combine all the ingredients.

2. Marinate the chicken and tofu overnight; the fish for 2–3 hours. Then fry in a griddle pan, barbecue or grill, according to taste. Serve with a fresh salad. Once marinated, this dish may be frozen in individual portions; defrost and cook as directed.

Simple Marinade for Beef, Lamb and Pork

1 tablespoon olive oil

1 teaspoon finely chopped ginger

1 garlic clove, crushed

1 teaspoon mustard

1 teaspoon crushed rosemary

salt and pepper

Makes enough for a 125–75g (4–6oz) portion of meat
Carbs 2.5g
Fat 14g
Protein trace

1. Combine all the ingredients.

2. Marinate the meat overnight, then fry in a griddle pan, barbecue or grill, according to taste. Serve with a fresh salad. Once marinated, the meat may be frozen in individual portions; defrost and cook as directed.

Weight ranges

Figures adapted from those provided by the Metropolitan Life Insurance Company, New York, 1959.

women

Height	1.45m	4 ft 9 in	1.65m	5 ft 5 in
Small frame	40.82 kg – 43.10 kg	90 lb – 97 lb	51.71 kg – 55.80 kg	114 lb – 123 lb
Medium frame	42.64 kg – 48.08 kg	94 lb – 106 lb	54.43 kg – 61.24 kg	120 lb – 135 lb
Large frame	46.27 kg – 53.52 kg	102 lb – 118 lb	58.51 kg – 66.23 kg	129 lb – 146 lb
Height	**1.47m**	**4 ft 10 in**	**1.68m**	**5 ft 6 in**
Small frame	41.73 kg – 45.36 kg	92 lb – 100 lb	53.52 kg – 57.61 kg	118 lb – 127 lb
Medium frame	43.10 kg – 49.44 kg	97 lb – 109 lb	56.25 kg – 63.05 kg	124 lb – 139 lb
Large frame	47.63 kg – 54.89 kg	105 lb – 121 lb	60.33 kg – 68.04 kg	133 lb – 150 lb
Height	**1.50m**	**4 ft 11 in**	**1.70m**	**5 ft 7 in**
Small frame	43.09 kg – 46.72 kg	95 lb – 103 lb	55.34 kg – 59.42 kg	122 lb – 131 lb
Medium frame	45.36 kg – 50.80 kg	100 lb – 112 lb	58.06 kg – 64.86 kg	128 lb – 143 lb
Large frame	48.99 kg – 56.25 kg	108 lb – 124 lb	62.14 kg – 69.85 kg	137 lb – 154 lb
Height	**1.52m**	**5 ft**	**1.72m**	**5 ft 8 in**
Small frame	44.45 kg – 48.08 kg	98 lb – 106 lb	57.15 kg – 61.69 kg	126 lb – 136 lb
Medium frame	46.72 kg – 52.16 kg	103 lb – 115 lb	59.88 kg – 66.68 kg	132 lb – 147 lb
Large frame	50.35 kg – 57.61 kg	111 lb – 127 lb	63.96 kg – 72.12 kg	141 lb – 159 lb
Height	**1.55m**	**5 ft 1 in**	**1.75m**	**5 ft 9 in**
Small frame	45.81 kg – 49.44 kg	101 lb – 109 lb	58.97 kg – 63.50 kg	130 lb – 140 lb
Medium frame	48.08 kg – 53.53 kg	106 lb – 118 lb	61.69 kg – 68.49 kg	136 lb – 151 lb
Large frame	51.71 kg – 58.97 kg	114 lb – 130 lb	65.77 kg – 74.39 kg	145 lb – 164 lb
Height	**1.57m**	**5 ft 2 in**	**1.78m**	**5 ft 10 in**
Small frame	47.17 kg – 50.80 kg	104 lb – 112 lb	60.33 kg – 65.32 kg	133 lb – 144 lb
Medium frame	49.44 kg – 55.34 kg	109 lb – 122 lb	58.97 kg – 70.31 kg	140 lb – 155 lb
Large frame	53.07 kg – 60.78 kg	117 lb – 134 lb	67.59 kg – 76.66 kg	149 lb – 169 lb
Height	**1.60m**	**5 ft 3 in**	**1.80m**	**5 ft 11 in**
Small frame	48.53 kg – 52.16 kg	107 lb – 115 lb	62.15 kg – 67.14 kg	137 lb – 147 lb
Medium frame	50.80 kg – 57.15 kg	112 lb – 126 lb	60.79 kg – 72.13 kg	147 lb – 159 lb
Large frame	54.89 kg – 62.60 kg	121 lb – 138 lb	69.41 kg – 78.48 kg	153 lb – 173 lb
Height	**1.63m**	**5 ft 4 in**	**1.83m**	**6 ft**
Small frame	49.70 kg – 53.98 kg	110 lb – 119 lb	63.97 kg – 68.96 kg	140 lb – 150 lb
Medium frame	52.62 kg – 59.42 kg	116 lb – 131 lb	62.61 kg – 73.95 kg	150 lb – 162 lb
Large frame	56.70 kg – 64.41 kg	125 lb – 142 lb	71.23 kg – 80.30 kg	156 lb – 176 lb

men

Height	1.55m	5 ft 1in	1.75m	5 ft 9 in
Small frame	47.63 kg – 51.26 kg	105 lb – 113 lb	60.33 kg – 64.87 kg	133 lb – 143 lb
Medium frame	50.35 kg – 55.34 kg	111 lb – 122 lb	63.05 kg – 69.40 kg	139 lb – 153 lb
Large frame	53.98 kg – 60.78 kg	119 lb – 134 lb	67.13 kg – 75.73 kg	148 lb – 167 lb
Height	**1.57m**	**5 ft 2in**	**1.78m**	**5 ft 10 in**
Small frame	48.99 kg – 52.62 kg	108 lb – 116 lb	62.14 kg – 66.68 kg	137 lb – 147 lb
Medium frame	51.71 kg – 57.15 kg	114 lb – 126 lb	64.86 kg – 71.67 kg	143 lb – 158 lb
Large frame	55.34 kg – 62.14 kg	122 lb – 137 lb	68.95 kg – 78.02 kg	152 lb – 172 lb
Height	**1.60m**	**5 ft 3 in**	**1.80 m**	**5 ft 11 in**
Small frame	50.35 kg – 53.98 kg	111 lb – 119 lb	63.96 kg – 68.49 kg	141 lb – 151 lb
Medium frame	53.07 kg – 58.51 kg	117 lb – 129 lb	66.68 kg – 73.94 kg	147 lb – 163 lb
Large frame	56.70 kg – 63.96 kg	125 lb – 141 lb	71.22 kg – 80.29 kg	157 lb – 177 lb
Height	**1.63m**	**5 ft 4 in**	**1.83m**	**6 ft**
Small frame	51.71 kg – 55.34 kg	114 lb – 122 lb	65.77 kg – 70.31 kg	145 lb – 155 lb
Medium frame	54.43 kg – 59.88 kg	120 lb – 132 lb	68.49 kg – 78.47 kg	151 lb – 173 lb
Large frame	58.06 kg – 65.77 kg	128 lb – 145 lb	75.30 kg – 84.82 kg	166 lb – 187 lb
Height	**1.65m**	**5 ft 5 in**	**1.85m**	**6 ft 1 in**
Small frame	53.07 kg – 57.15 kg	117 lb – 126 lb	67.59 kg – 72.58 kg	149 lb – 160 lb
Medium frame	55.79 kg – 61.69 kg	123 lb – 136 lb	70.31 kg – 78.47 kg	155 lb – 173 lb
Large frame	59.42 kg – 67.59 kg	131 lb – 149 lb	75.30 kg – 84.82 kg	166 lb – 187 lb
Height	**1.68m**	**5 ft 6 in**	**1.88m**	**6 ft 2 in**
Small frame	54.89 kg – 58.97 kg	121 lb – 130 lb	69.40 kg – 74.39 kg	153 lb – 164 lb
Medium frame	57.61 kg – 63.50 kg	127lb – 140 lb	72.58 kg – 80.74 kg	160 lb – 178 lb
Large frame	61.24 kg – 69.85 kg	135lb – 154 lb	77.57 kg – 87.09 kg	171 lb – 192 lb
Height	**1.70m**	**5 ft 7 in**	**1.90m**	**6 ft 3 in**
Small frame	56.70 kg – 60.78 kg	125 lb – 134 lb	71.21 kg – 76.21 kg	157 lb – 168 lb
Medium frame	59.42 kg – 65.77 kg	131 lb – 145 lb	74.84 kg – 83.01 kg	165 lb – 183 lb
Large frame	63.50 kg – 72.12 kg	140 lb – 159 lb	79.38 kg – 89.36 kg	175 lb – 197 lb
Height	**1.72m**	**5 ft 8 in**	**1.92m**	**6 ft 4 in**
Small frame	58.51 kg – 62.60 kg	129 lb – 138 lb	73.02 kg – 78.02 kg	161 lb – 172 lb
Medium frame	61.24 kg – 67.59 kg	135 lb – 149 lb	76.65 kg – 84.82 kg	169 lb – 187 lb
Large frame	65.32 kg – 73.94 kg	144 lb – 163 lb	81.19 kg – 91.17 kg	179 lb – 201 lb

Index

Acknowledgements

Acknowledgements in Source Order

Octopus Publishing Group Limited /Frank Adam 3 left, 3 right, 8, 11 left, 11 right, 11 centre, 16, 17, 19, 20, 21 top right, 21 bottom left, 22, 23 left, 23 right, 23 centre, 26, 27 top left, 27 top right, 27 bottom, 28 top, 28 bottom, 31, 32, 33, 39 left, 39 right, 39 centre, 40, 49, 50 left, 50 centre, 51 right, 55, 60, 62, 65, 66, 69, 71, 73, 77, 79, 80, 82, 85, 86, 87, 89, 96, 99, 100, 103, 104, 106, 108, 109, 111, 113, 114, 115, 116, 119, **/Sandra Lane** 7, 12, 18, **/David Loftus** 64, **/Sean Myers** 68, **/William Reavell** 81, **/Simon Smith** 13.

Photodisc 3 centre, 15, 34, 35, 36, 37, 44, 46.

Commissioning Editor: Nicola Hill
Editor: Clare Churley
Executive Art Editor: Geoff Fennell
Designer: Martin Topping
Photography: Frank Adam
Food Stylist: David Morgan
Stylist: Angela Swaffield
Picture Researcher: Jennifer Veall
Production Controller: Viv Cracknell